Gender, Class and Reflexive Modernity in India

Genders and Sexualities in the Social Sciences
Series Standing Order ISBN 978–0–230–27254–5 hardback
978–0–230–27255–2 paperback
(*outside North America only*)

You can receive future titles in this series as they are published by placing a standing order. Please contact your bookseller or, in case of difficulty, write to us at the address below with your name and address, the title of the series and the ISBN quoted above.

Customer Services Department, Macmillan Distribution Ltd., Houndmills, Basingstoke, Hampshire RG21 6XS, England

Gender, Class and Reflexive Modernity in India

Jyothsna Latha Belliappa
Azim Premji University, India

First published 2013 by
PALGRAVE MACMILLAN

Palgrave Macmillan in the UK is an imprint of Macmillan Publishers Limited, registered in England, company number 785998, of Houndmills, Basingstoke, Hampshire RG21 6XS.

Palgrave Macmillan in the US is a division of St Martin's Press LLC, 175 Fifth Avenue, New York, NY 10010.

Palgrave Macmillan is the global academic imprint of the above companies and has companies and representatives throughout the world.

Palgrave® and Macmillan® are registered trademarks in the United States, the United Kingdom, Europe and other countries.

ISBN 978–0–230–30018–7

This book is printed on paper suitable for recycling and made from fully managed and sustained forest sources. Logging, pulping and manufacturing processes are expected to conform to the environmental regulations of the country of origin.

A catalogue record for this book is available from the British Library.

A catalog record for this book is available from the Library of Congress.

Typeset by MPS Limited, Chennai, India.

For Diana, Deepa and Krithika

Contents

List of Tables

Acknowledgements

The research for this book was completed with the help of financial assistance from the University of York, UK, the Lady Meherbai Tata Trust, the British Federation of Women Graduates and the Lotus Trust of India. I am deeply grateful for their generosity. In addition to financial support, a research project of this nature requires the support of many people across different continents. I am indebted to the anonymous women whose accounts form the basis of this book, who generously shared with me their most precious resource, their time. I hope I have done justice to their accounts and their enthusiasm for my project. I am also grateful to many others who, under conditions of anonymity, shared personal anecdotes that first alerted me to the questions that inform this project.

The research began at the Centre for Women's Studies (CWS) at the University of York. I am indebted to Professors Stevi Jackson and Haleh Afshar and to the staff at CWS, Dr Ann Kaloski-Naylor and Professor Gabrielle Griffin and Harriet Badger, for their unstinting personal and academic support. I also thank Professor Bhikhu Parekh for his valuable advice on my work.

Back in India, Dr Geetha Narayanan and my colleagues at Srishti School of Art, Design and Technology welcomed a social scientist and her project into a creative melting pot of artists, designers, activists and scholars. I thank my colleagues Sathish Jayarajan and Vandana Goswami for intellectual support, Ajai Narendra for patiently following up on all my requests for references and Swami and Geeta for being such cheerful and helpful librarians. Thanks are also due to Manini Menon for help with indexing and to Beena Ullal, Manjul Menon and Aruna Chidambi for proofreading the manuscript. That said, the responsibility for any mistakes in this book, typographical or otherwise, is solely mine!

My sincere gratitude to the editorial team at Palgrave Macmillan, especially Philippa Grand, Andrew James and Naomi Robinson, for their support and gracious responses to every request for an 'extension'. Equally sincere thanks are due to Professor Rajeev Gowda and Professor M. N. Panini in India and to Dr Linda Perriton and Dr Anne Akeroyd in Britain who are never too busy to offer advice, support and humour. I also thank the anonymous reviewer whose thoughtful suggestions have strengthened my arguments and conclusions.

My heartfelt gratitude to friends in Bangalore, Anupama Mahajan, Monisha Srichand and Anita Rajnarayan, for their support, and to my 'transatlantic support system', Diana Peters, Deepa Parija and Krithika Jagannath and their wonderful families. Finally, I thank my grandparents, Late Sri Baliamada B. Kushalappa and Srimati Sita Kushalappa, who have had more influence on this book than they can imagine.

1
Setting Out to Study Class and Gender in Contemporary India

While there are many ways for a scholar to choose a topic for research, it occasionally happens that the topic of research chooses the scholar. Usually this occurs when a setting or community which is familiar to the scholar begins to show signs of rapid change. I first began asking the questions addressed in this book at the turn of the century when my hometown, Bangalore, a quiet city in southern India, became the nerve centre of India's burgeoning information technology (IT) industry. My friends and neighbours went to work for large multinational corporations at unprecedented salaries; international brands of soft drinks, apparel and white goods appeared on the shelves of neighbourhood stores; and people started remarking on how India had arrived on the world stage. Bangalore, the administrative capital of the peninsular state of Karnataka, affectionately nicknamed 'pensioner's paradise' due to its slow pace of life, came to be known as India's 'Silicon Valley'.

A clamour of voices arose around me – some excited, optimistic, eager to be part of the new, globalized India that our city had come to represent; others cautious, fearing that our society would be polarized between those who could benefit from the opportunities that globalization creates and those who were marginalized by it; still others angry, aggressive – clamouring for protecting our culture and heritage from what they viewed as the decadence of the West. Several of these voices mentioned women: 'women will benefit most from the new opportunities created by the free-market economy'; 'women have begun to embrace change ahead of men'; 'women will preserve our culture in the face of globalization'; 'women need to be protected from corrupt Western influences'. This book began as an attempt to hear, over the clamour of these multiple and contradictory voices, the voices of women themselves. Quite early on I decided to zero in on women

1

employed in the IT industry, to question how those women who are constructed as representatives and beneficiaries of India's economic growth story understand their experiences.

Over the past seven years I have carried first my questions and later my tentative answers into conferences and seminars, informal discussions with colleagues and the occasional dinner party with friends. While some of my initial naive hopes that my questions will lead to unambiguous answers have been shed, the aim of understanding how women make sense of their experiences rather than using their experiences as raw data to be theorized remains strong. I have also begun to see my research as a small part of a larger feminist project: that of raising questions about mainstream sociology. Therefore while this book is born of a qualitative research project on middle class Indian women employed in the global economy, its broader aim is to contribute to a Southern feminist perspective within the ongoing critique of reflexive modernity within sociology.

A Southern feminist project

The project of Southern feminism is not new – over the past twenty years a significant body of theoretical and empirical work has been developed around women of the Global South. Much has been said in favour of understanding women's experiences in the Global South and against monochromatic perspectives of non-White/Southern/non-Western/ peripheral/marginal women offered by White/mainstream/Western feminists located in the Global North/western hemisphere/centre (see, for example, Bulbeck, 1998; Trinh, 1989; Mohanty, 1984; Narayan, 2000). It has been argued that as a result of centering the concerns and perspectives of southern women, feminism has become more inclusive and critical, engaging with wider concerns such as racism, communalism and poverty.

Thirty years ago Chandra Talpade Mohanty (1984) contended that much of the predominantly White, Western/First World scholarship on non-White or non-Western women tends to take a reductionist approach, constructing the 'average' Asian, Black or Third World woman as a monolithic entity usually characterized by victimhood. She argued for an understanding of non-White or non-Western women that was located in real lived experiences of women in material and structural conditions of disempowerment or disenfranchisement and in the historical, cultural and geographical specificities of local contexts. Moreover, she argued, the very categories of Asian women, Arab women or Third World women may obliterate the class, ethnic and religious diversities within the societies they represent, a view echoed by Chilla Bulbeck (1998). While Mohanty's terminological classification of First and Third Worlds and Bulbeck's West and East may not always be appropriate, their ideas continue to remain relevant. In this book I take inspiration from the call of these and other Southern feminists to study the day-to-day lived experiences of *one specific group* of Southern women in their local context and understand how they negotiate and resist hegemonic gendered values.

By focussing on an economically relatively privileged group that nevertheless faces marginalization and discrimination in professional life, and contends with traditional constraints in family life, I query the constructions of Southern women as victims of religious orthodoxies, patriarchal families and global capitalist interests. I attempt to change the angle from Southern women as recipients of help from international donors to Southern women as economic agents. Drawing attention to the consequences of neoliberalism and global capitalism, I investigate how access to economic opportunities influences women's sense of self. In the 19th century, social reformer *Pandita*[1] Ramabai argued that the lack of opportunities for middle class/upper caste women to practise self-reliance is a key issue in their oppression (Pandita Ramabai/Kosambi, 1888/2000). The *Pandita's* assertion alerts us to two important ideas: that middle class women's experiences do not represent an average or universal by which we can draw conclusions about gender relations across society and that economic privileges do not always translate into empowerment for women.

The university educated English-speaking women represented in this study are in a unique position as workers: their education gives them access to what might seem like relatively well-paid jobs in the trans-national IT (software) industry, but their location within the global labour market makes them vulnerable to economic shifts and changes. Although they work in luxurious environments and enjoy higher incomes than others with comparable experience in less prestigious industries, they have limited means of negotiating working conditions, compensation, hours and benefits with transnational employers and clients. The acclaim that they receive in the media, in popular discourse and in their families for their participation in the global economy and their position as representatives of India's new status as an economic power masks their vulnerability in the face of global capital. Yet the constraints that they face are very different from non-literate, poorer women employed in other global industries such as the garment industry or transnational domestic workers.

This book investigates, through first-person accounts, how these women understand the complexities of their positions in the professional sphere and in their families. While acknowledging the importance of studying the lives of women who are oppressed by caste, class and religious hierarchies, it contends that not all Southern women are oppressed or even marginalized in the same way. Moreover, it argues that India's (economic) growth story needs to be problematized and examined through the lenses of gender and class. By querying middle class discourses, it attempts to further emerging trends in self-reflexivity amongst Indian sociologists and social anthropologists.

It also addresses, indirectly, what might be called a crisis in Indian feminism (echoed by other feminisms across the world, see Scharff, 2011; McRobbie, 2009; Rich, 2005). As Chapter 3 will argue, the contemporary women's movement has a long history in India dating at least to the 19th century. Many middle class/upper caste women participated in the nationalist movement in the 19th and early 20th centuries, seeking women's liberation in conjunction with the nation's independence. In independent India, a robust women's movement grew in the 1970s and early 1980s. This time women's rights were sought independently from other political issues, resulting in the label 'autonomous women's movement'. In both phases, the movement was largely dominated by educated, urban, middle class women, leading to accusations of elitism and suggestions that middle class leaders of the movement had appropriated the right to speak on behalf of their less privileged 'sisters' (Rege, 1998; Agnes, 1994). In spite of these somewhat justified accusations, it might be argued that these early feminists of pre- and post-independent India were motivated by a strong sense of commitment to a wider social and political cause and, in many cases, a willingness to support women who were additionally marginalized by caste, poverty or rural location.

Several political events and circumstances undermined the feminist cause in the 1990s and at the turn of the century, including the active participation of elite and middle class women in the anti-Mandal commission agitation which saw upper castes violently opposing affirmative action towards lower castes and classes. Women played key roles in right-wing religious movements and communal conflicts, including the demolition of the Babri Masjid and the violence against Muslims in Mumbai in 1993 and Gujarat in 2002. These issues have given rise to grave concerns amongst veteran feminists that the cause of women's liberation is challenged by conflicting allegiances in terms of caste, religion and political affiliation (Agnes, 1994; Agnihotri and Mazumdar,

1995; Tharu and Niranjana, 1996; Padke, 2003). But a more steady and insidious erosion of the feminist movement amongst the middle classes seems to have occurred with the advance of neoliberalism.

Feminists in Britain such as McRobbie (2009) and Scharff (2011) argue that neoliberalism offers possibilities of emancipation and autonomy not through collective action but through individual effort. The women whose accounts inform this book seek autonomy, independence and self-determination through sustained individual effort, carefully planned choices and strategic conformity to traditional norms. There is little evidence of their commitment to a larger social or political cause, feminist or otherwise. This book analyses their engagement with neoliberal ideals of choice and empowerment, thereby indirectly suggesting some reasons behind their disengagement with feminism.

A word on terminology: over the past few decades, many binary terms have been used to describe cultures across the world: First World and Third World, centre and periphery, West and non-West and more recently Global North and Global South. All these classifications carry the possibility of reducing diversity in cultures to a small number of essentialized traits. In an increasingly interlinked world where people, goods and ideas flow in multiple directions, such binary categories can become unproductive and limiting; they might conceal internal diversities and contradictions. Yet it is necessary to use some categories whilst acknowledging with Trinh T. Minh-ha (1989: 94) that 'despite our desperate eternal attempt to contain and mend, categories always leak'. Amongst the various terms I have chosen to use in this book are the Global South and Global North which indicate the structural inequities and cultural differences between cultures, societies and nations of the northern and southern hemispheres whilst acknowledging the presence of prosperous nations in the South and relatively poor nations in the North. However when quoting writers who employ a different set of binaries, I use their terminology rather than my own. This might be confusing for the reader, but I see no other way of preserving the authenticity of their arguments.

The challenges of the 'insider' position in the south

Trinh T. Min-ha (1989) argues that although Third World feminists are increasingly visible in First World forums, their participation is often circumscribed by certain implicit and explicit expectations: that they will represent their culture authentically (the judgement of this authenticity is usually in the hands of powerful First World academies), that they will enable their First World colleagues to understand and experience difference, that they will refrain from engaging with First World issues. Her views resonate with feminist academics from Asia, Africa and Latin America who are usually expected to represent the predominant view of their culture. Such expectations overlook the diversity within societies and cultures, the multiple political positions that individual feminists might take on their own culture and their capacity to comment on cultures other than their own.

The Southern feminist academic researching her own culture then stands under a double-edged sword. On the one hand she might see great value in researching and representing her own culture either in an attempt to challenge the myths and fallacies of previous representations or with the goal of representing an under-represented subject. On the other hand she risks being seen as a native informant offering an exotic 'Other' to mainstream Northern subjects. In my experience this paradoxical position further is complicated by pressure from within my home culture to provide an authentic (read: positive) account of Indian women to audiences abroad. This pressure was particularly evident when research participants would ask repeatedly, 'Do you understand what I am saying?' or instruct, 'This is what you need to say about Indian women.' These dual pressures from within and outside her culture position the Southern feminist researcher as either native informant or ambassador. Both positions presume a certain expertise on 'the field' and are ethically suspect since they suggest that 'insider' status directly translates into superior knowledge about the culture.

Mohanty (1984), Narayan (2000) and other Southern feminists warn White, Western scholars about the dangers of cultural essentialism in studying non-White, non-Western women. However, the same warning might be given to Southern researchers who may be tempted to present over-essentialized pictures of their cultures in response to the myths and fallacies about their cultures that they encounter in their academic and social environments. Southern feminists are in no less danger than other academics of reinscribing 'the researched into prevailing representations' of victimhood or deviance (Bhavnani, 1994: 30), constructing research participants as victims (Mohanty, 1984; Narayan, 2000) of their cultures, of patriarchal families and of global capitalism. Such a position denies their ability to negotiate with their families, their capacity to challenge power structures and their sense of agency. The reverse trap would be to construct 'heroine stories', celebrating the success and empowerment of Indian women in the global economy. Both forms of essentialization close off analytical possibilities by masking complexities within cultures and disguising how power is exchanged, bartered, withheld and deployed in given contexts.

Whilst recognizing and theorizing differences between and within ethnic and national communities, Southern researchers also need to recognize that uncritical uses of difference lead to another pitfall – that of obliterating the similarities between cultures in different geographical locations, especially those that confronted each other in unequal relations of colonialism. The tendency of each power to create an identity in opposition to the Other obliterates '[p]rofound *similarities* between Western culture and many of its Others, such as hierarchical social systems, huge economic disparities between members, and the mistreatment and inequality of women' (Narayan, 2000: 84, italics in original). In this study cautious comparisons with other cultures have helped me to recognize similarities in women's experiences of work-life collision, motherhood and individualization across the globe. Narayan's argument is even more relevant than when she made it ten years ago, given the multiple linkages between cultures and nations across the globe, the interactions between people across transnational spaces, mediatization and digitization of public life and the close relationships between national economies. This study therefore upholds a position of 'difference' which, to paraphrase Trinh T. (1989), carries creative possibilities of both difference and sameness, but not difference as a synonym for a separate and authentic non-White 'self'.

Research participants: Self-selected, eager and enthusiastic

The twenty-six women whose accounts inform this book were interviewed via semi-structured interviews and two focus groups between 2006 and 2007. They are employed in various functions in the IT industry, including administration, software engineering, finance, human resources and technical writing. All of them worked with well-established multinational IT (software and software services) companies, including both offshore development centres of major foreign companies and Indian multinationals that had a transnational presence. Both women in management-track positions and non-management-track positions were interviewed. The women were aged between twenty-four and thirty-seven years at the time of the interviews. Of these twenty-three were married, two were single and one was going through marital separation and divorce. Sixteen of the married women had either one or two children (the prevalent norm amongst Indian middle class families). Considering that the mean age for marriage in India is 19.5 years the large number of married women is not surprising. Brief profiles of all interviewees are recorded in the appendix.

There is considerable diversity amongst the research participants in terms of social background: between them they represent about seven different linguistic groups; eleven of them are from the south of India and five from the North; fourteen explicitly identified as Hindu, three identified as Christian and one as Muslim. The remaining eight did not indicate their religion. None of the Hindus belonged to the depressed castes. While I do not claim to have recruited a representative sample for the study, the smaller proportion of religious minorities and the absence of depressed castes amongst my participants reflect their poor representation in the industry (Upadhya and Vasavi, 2006), an issue that is discussed in Chapter 4.

Interviews lasted for an average of 2 to 2½ hours. They were conducted in English, the language of business communication in India. However the interviewees' fluency in the language is considerably varied as the quotes from the interviews will indicate. To preserve the authenticity of their accounts, no attempt has been made to 'clean up' quotes or translate them into colloquial English, though some quotes may be shortened for lack of space. In such cases, ellipses are used to indicate the missing text. Since quotes are otherwise verbatim, they often contain grammatical errors and unfinished sentences, indicated by a dash. As with most communication in India, English is supplemented with words from vernacular languages (in this case Hindi and Kannada, the national and regional languages) which have been translated for the reader.

Although I considered contacting interviewees through the human resource departments of various IT companies, I finally decided to use personal contacts in the IT industry and find interviewees through a snowballing method. This method worked well as interviewees inevitably introduced me to their friends and colleagues, thereby soon taking my network much beyond my initial contacts. Being introduced in this manner enabled me to win interviewees' trust and confidence more easily. I was perceived as a friend of a friend rather than as someone connected with the authorities. Women indicated that they became interested in being interviewed on hearing from friends that the experience of being interviewed had been interesting or satisfying. Many women said that they were glad their personal experiences would contribute to a wider purpose.

In addition to 'personalized credibility', it also helped to have some 'impersonal credibility' through my affiliation to a research centre within an international university. I often followed up my initial contact by emailing interviewees a link to my research abstract on the university's webpage. Some interviewees read the project abstract before the interview and asked specific questions, but for most of them it was enough to know that I was a doctoral student at an established university. Since the interviewees were a self-selected group, they were usually eager to participate. Many expressed a desire to see the research in print, arguing that the story of India's transformation into a globalized economy and their own experiences of this transformation was indeed interesting and meaningful, a story that needs to be told. Their enthusiasm and encouragement left me feeling both humbled and grateful. I hope I have done justice to them in this book.

Looking at the middle classes

In her book *Liberating Method*, Marjorie DeVault (1999: 25) argues that a major task of academic feminism is 'talking back to (conventional) Sociology' by raising questions not only about methodology and epistemology but also by destabilizing the grand meta-narratives of sociology and 'excavating' subjects and perspectives that have hitherto been ignored or suppressed. This book is an attempt to cut through popular rhetoric about women's positions in contemporary India by examining their subjective experiences of class, modernity and globalization. In doing so it explores a subject that has received scant attention in Indian sociology.

Although it is several years since I took my first degree, I vividly recall my first exposure to sociology as an undergraduate student in India. While we had many stimulating discussions around caste, gender, politics and religion, I do not remember a single lecture, seminar or discussion on the Indian middle classes, that section of Indian society to which we students and the lecturers who taught us belonged. Satish Deshpande (2003: 128) attributes the reluctance to study the middle class for much of the 20th century to the notion that it seems an '"unworthy" or self indulgent [subject] for a generation of [Indian] social scientists drawn from this class, who believed that their mandate was to act on behalf of "the people" who constituted the nation'. When we ignore the middle class, however, we are in danger of unconsciously and uncritically adopting its worldview and overlooking its role in promoting dominant discourses on gender, modernity and nationhood. To achieve a deeper understanding of how these discourses are created and strengthened, it is important to undertake empirical work on the middle classes.

Though social scientists might have ignored the middle classes, they continued to play an influential role in the nation – first as participants in the nationalist movement; later as small-scale entrepreneurs, white-collar workers and government servants; and recently as supporters of economic deregulation. From the mid-1980s, successive governments addressed the middle classes not only as a vote bank but also as an economic resource for the nation. In the absence of ethnographic research, other forms of scholarship on the middle classes emerged at the turn of the century.

Pavan Varma's (1998) *Great Indian Middle Class* and Dipankar Gupta's (2000) *Mistaken Modernity* both argue that the Indian middle classes are quite narrowly focussed on their own self-interest. Gupta's idea of 'westoxification' (a term he attributes to the Iranian intellectual Jalal-e-Ahmed) expressively describes the middle class's preoccupation with electronic gadgetry, foreign brands and other trappings of modernity. He contends that the middle class continues to follow many traditional practices and that its privilege is based on several traditional and inegalitarian structures. Varma argues that with economic deregulation in 1991, Gandhian austerity and Nehruvian socialism gave way to an ideology that consumption is beneficial to the nation. While both arguments are compelling, what is missing from these writings are the voices of the middle classes themselves and, as Favero (2005: 134) argues, 'a lack of self-reflexivity and middle class self-identification [which] unites the authors I have mentioned with their audience'.

Varma's assertion that the middle class is 'morally rudderless, obsessively materialistic, and socially insensitive to the point of being unconcerned with anything but its own narrow self-interest' reflects a highly self-critical discourse amongst sections of the middle class. In contrast, Gurucharan Das's view is more self-congratulatory. In his *India Unbound* he suggests that India has indeed arrived on the world stage, that the entrepreneurial spirit of the middle classes which was shackled by government regulation has finally been unleashed, and that the new-found prosperity of the middle classes will percolate across society. This view enjoys high purchase in the media and popular discourse. What is required, however, is a sociological examination of the middle class, which distances itself from both self-recrimination and self-congratulation (Béteille, 2001).

In the 21st century, social scientists have begun to interrogate the burgeoning popular and corporate discourse on the Indian middle classes (see Fernandes, 2006; Deshpande, 2003; Gupta, 2000; Favero, 2005 Upadhya and Vasavi, 2006; Jafferlot and Van der Veer, 2008; Tim

Scrase and Rita Ganguly-Scrase, 2009). For instance Favero's (2005) ethnography on young men's experiences of identity creation within urban India is useful in understanding how individuals attempt to create a sense of self within globalization. Upadhya and Vasavi's (2006) indepth ethnography of the IT industry investigates the new subclass of IT professionals that is located within contradictions of the local and the global. Scrase and Ganguly-Scrase (2009) examine the opportunities and challenges created by the globalization for lower middle class men and women in Kolkota. Fernandes (2006) considers how the 'new' middle class is both discursively and structurally created, and Deshpande (2003) examines through both an economist's and a sociologist's lens whether the middle class is really the class in the middle of the social hierarchy. Van der Veer and Jafferlot (2008) consider different forms of consumption within the middle classes in two emerging economies: India and China. However while many of these titles have a chapter or two on gender, they are not directly concerned with women.

One of the main conceptual struggles shared by sociologists of the middle classes is the difficulty in defining the term (Deshpande, 2003; Jafferlot and Van der Veer, 2008; Ray and Baviskar, 2011). Ray and Baviskar (2011) suggest that this is because middle classes are at once the elite as well as 'everybody' (given the popularity of the identity for self-definition). In both scholarly discussion and popular speech, the term is used with a 'taken-for-grantedness' which makes it hard to pin down, yet both reader and writer seem to understand who is being referred to. The category itself is very broad in terms of income, requiring the use of the plural 'middle classes' in many instances. In this book I adapt the National Council of Applied Economic Research's (NCAER) (2005) consumer categories to include in the middle class households earning between US$3684.60 and US$36846 per annum. In 2011 the NCAER suggested that middle classes would be in the income bracket of US$5526.90 to US$31319.10, but given that interviews for this research occurred between 2006 and 2007, it is appropriate to use their 2005 classification.

While the category of middle class may be sub-divided economically into upper, middle and lower strata, middle class identity is not only based on income. In Chapter 3, I argue that there are certain social indicators of middle class status, including the desire to acquire, accumulate and deploy cultural capital in order to strengthen and enhance one's class status. However, at this stage it is important to mention that all the women I interviewed self-identified as middle class. Based on the feminist principles of this work, which privilege the frameworks of individual women alongside academic theory, I accepted this self-identification, probing it further to arrive at an understanding of where they might be located in the middle class, that is, at the upper, middle or lower levels. All the women interviewed belong either to the middle or the upper middle class; that is, they have a household income of Rs 500,000 to 1,000,000 (or US$10,000 to US$40,000). Most interviewees have moved up from the income category below the one they currently inhabit, that is, from 'lower middle class' to 'middle middle class' or from 'middle middle' to 'upper middle class', through the opportunities available in the global economy.

Emerging ethnography on middle class women

As I argued in the previous section, there has been, till recently, little work on the middle classes and even less on middle class women. However, a few exceptions exist, which include the work of Jyoti Puri (1999), Purnima Mankekar (1999), Meenakshi Thapan, (2004), Rupal Oza (2006), J.K. Tina Basi (2009) and Smitha Radhakrishnan (2011). Earlier work on women and class includes that of Joanna Liddle and Rama Joshi (1986) and Patricia Caplan (1985). Oza (2006) examines how economic liberalization, the consolidation of the middle classes and the rise of the Hindu right have influenced the relationship between gender and nationalism in contemporary India, while Thapan (2004) investigates the discursive constructions of the 'new' Indian (middle and upper class) woman. Both argue that the perceived vulnerability of national sovereignty in the face of global capitalism is displaced onto the bodies and sexualities of woman. Women's bodies and behaviours are policed with a view to protect their purity from the 'sexual permissiveness' of global culture. At the same time the identity of the 'new' Indian women is constituted to include education, professional qualifications, paid employment and the ability to choose and consume products in the global market alongside commitment to home, husband and children. Women's identities are believed to be constituted of a 'respectable modernity enshrined in tradition' (Thapan, 2004: 415).

Ethnographic research undertaken amongst middle class women supports Thapan's and Oza's conclusions but also indicates how individuals might resist dominant discursive constructions of Indian womanhood. Mankekar's (1999) investigation of audiences' engagement with representations of gender, identity, nationhood and modernity on state-sponsored television in a middle class neighbourhood in New Delhi found that narratives of modernity contained within tradition were fairly entrenched. Barring a few exceptions, viewers by and large accepted the visual narratives of television wherein women exercised their individual agency for the family, community or nation rather than themselves. She argues that rising consumerism fuelled demands for dowry and required women to engage more widely in paid employment, but these trends did not necessarily influence women to seek independence from marriage and family.

Puri (1999) investigates narratives of sexuality, menstruation, marriage and motherhood amongst middle class women in Mumbai to analyse how dominant codes of gender, heteronormativity and sexual respectability serve to restrict women's sexuality and freedom. She argues that not only do lived experiences indicate how hegemonic codes of gender and sexuality are naturalized but also how these codes might be disrupted by individual agency. In Chapter 3, I draw attention to some parallels between her findings on marriage and motherhood and my own.

There is also a growing body of work on women in the call centre/BPO industry. J.K. Tina Basi (2009) explores women's subjective experiences of call centre work in New Delhi to conclude that the identities they construct confound conventional wisdom about exploitation by multinationals and the notion that outsourcing is the 'colonies' revenge'. She suggests that women's agency finds expression within and beyond the restrictions imposed by global capitalism and their own families. Both Puri and Basi suggest that while women's lives are deeply influenced and often restricted by dominant normative codes, they also, from time to time, resist the same codes that curtail their freedom and agency. In addition, they also find ways to use the same normative codes to their advantage crucially to gain protection and prestige from their observance of these codes.

In-depth ethnographic work on the IT industry is reported in Carol Upadhya and A.R. Vasavi's (2006) *Work, Culture and Sociality in the Indian IT Industry*; however, only a small portion of their report considers gender. While I draw on many of their insights in this book, I attempt to turn the ethnographic lens specifically on women who are employed in the IT industry. In this respect my work has some parallels with Radhakrishnan's (2011a) ethnography of the IT industry. As Radhakrishnan has argued, IT careers are highly prized due to the prestige that the industry has acquired for bringing transnational capital into India and its image as a conscientious and caring employer. The nature of work in the IT industry, its location on the frontiers of national boundaries and the transnational capitalist economy and the emergence of IT workers as an upwardly mobile and influential subclass make it a significant area of study. It is important to investigate the industry's claim (supported and endorsed in the popular press) that it fosters a highly conducive work environment for women and promotes the needs of its female employees through its human resource policies, by exploring women's own accounts of their experiences in the industry.

Radhakrishnan's suggestion that employees participate in the construction of the industry's egalitarian and meritocratic image, taking pride in its position as a key figure in India's globalization story, is borne out by my research, as is her argument that women in the IT industry embody a form of respectable femininity, proudly carrying markers of their Indianess into their high-tech, globalized work environments. However, my research will indicate that the strong alignment with the values of the industry that Radhakrishnan found is evident mainly amongst employees in the management track. Employees who are in administrative and support functions are more ambivalent about the industry's claim to being an egalitarian and caring employer. A few female managers who have experienced the double standards in the work-life balance rhetoric and the reality of the long-hours culture also raise questions about the industry's commitment to gender equality (see Chapter 5).

In addition to highlighting the internal diversity within the middle classes and its relationship with gender, this book examines how women make sense of the changes in their personal and professional lives by drawing on available cultural discourses. It is not only an ethnographic study on the experiences of middle class women who are believed to have benefited from globalization. A major aim of this book is to interrogate the reflexive modernity thesis attributed to Anthony Giddens and Ulrich Beck. In some ways the arguments of the reflexive modernity thesis may suggest how we might understand the nature of work and sociality in the IT industry and the changes that it has led to in Bangalore. However, as I argue in the empirical chapters, it does not explain many contradictions in women's experience of reflexive modernity and fails to account for individuals' creative strategies for overcoming these contradictions. It also overlooks the social nature of reflexivity. However, before turning to this part of my argument, it is necessary to understand the context in which research participants live and work. Therefore, in the following sections I briefly describe the growth of the IT industry and the city of Bangalore.

The IT industry

While conventional wisdom suggests that the IT industry has grown as a result of the deregulation of the Indian economy in 1991, a deeper investigation reveals that policies that supported technological growth and privatization of industry were established in the 1980s. In the years following independence, India followed a largely socialist economic policy based on state control of trade and industry, import substitution and large public sector and centralized planning. It is argued that this form of socialism limited consumption, encouraged individual and household savings and protected domestic industry from foreign competition (Varma, 1998). In the late 1980s, however, the then Prime Minister Rajiv Gandhi outlined his vision for a strong nation established on the basis of 'high technology, managerial efficiency and global economic competitiveness' (Fernandes, 2006: 35). Gandhi recognized the middle classes' appetite for consumption, supporting it through tax breaks and impetus to the television and automobile industries (Fernandes, 2006; Upadhya and Vasavi, 2006). During his regime the penetration of consumer goods such as televisions, VCRs and washing machines grew considerably. He also supported the growth of technology and the development of education via the National Policy on Education, 1986, which made provisions for the consolidation of technical and management education across the country. In this manner, the stage was set for the deregulation of the economy in 1991.

In response to a balance of payments crisis in 1991, the Indian government applied for a loan to the International Monetary Fund; the conditions of the loan required far-reaching economic reforms. While the then Prime Minister Narasimha Rao and Finance Minister Manmohan Singh initiated neoliberal reforms, successive governments continued the process, resulting in deregulation of the economy, increased privatization of key industries, reduction in duties on imports and impetus to foreign investment. India thus became integrated into the global free-market economy.

Several industries saw unprecedented growth as a result of 'economic liberalization': the services sector, banking, biotechnology and consumer goods. Telecommunication, airlines and other public sector industries were privatized, leading to increased competition and lower prices. The flagship industry of globalization in India is the IT industry. The IT industry's emblematic status may be due to the fact that along with the business process outsourcing industry it contributes to about 6.4% of the nation's GDP and about 26% of the nation's exports (National Association of Software and Services Companies (NASSCOM), 2010). It generates direct employment for about 2.5 million people (and indirectly employs over 8 million) of which at least 30% are women. The IT software and services sector accounts for US$76.1 billion of revenues.

The globally networked software industry, with its modernist buildings, unprecedented salaries and claims of a meritocratic ethos, is perceived as symbolic of a prosperous India that has shaken off the effects of colonialism and taken its rightful place in the world economy.

The IT industry's propaganda suggests that its growth may be attributed to the hard work of a few visionary entrepreneurs, the availability of a large talented and skilled English-speaking workforce, the growth of the services sector in the West and the consequent need for skilled workers. Upadhya and Vasavi (2006) argue that the state played a major role in supporting the industry through tax breaks, the creation of special economic zones and subsidies on land and infrastructure. Even at the regional governments such as the government of Karnataka provided land and tax holidays to support industrial growth. The central and state governments have a close consultative relationship with the NASSCOM, which acts both as industry representative and watchdog.

In keeping with this image, IT companies create infrastructure reminiscent of New York, Singapore and Dubai. The offices where I visited research participants have state-of-the-art facilities, concierge desks and swimming pools. They are equipped with superior quality electronic equipment, ergonomically designed furniture, even bean bags and couches. Cafeterias serve Indian, Chinese and American fast foods at subsidized rates. Many IT companies are housed in large, self-contained tech parks which also house restaurants, food courts, banks and sports facilities. There are elaborate security arrangements which further alienated them from the rest of the city. The remarks of the CEO of one company best exemplifies the image that the IT companies attempt to create: 'We like to think of Infosys [a major Indian company with transnational links] as *in India but not run by India* ... our clients should not notice that the infrastructure is any different to their own no matter where they come from' (Ramesh, 2000, in Sklair, 2001: 30–31, emphasis mine). It seems that even employees are made to feel that they are in another world far removed from the squalor, poverty and chaos that is an integral part of Bangalore's landscape.

The industry is also known for its progressive human resource policies and is considered a trendsetter in this area for other services industries. Employee engagement activities include celebrating festivals in the office, organizing parties and junkets, treks, music concerts, clubs and sports activities. Many offices have leisure centres equipped with large-screen televisions and hi-fi equipment where employees can view films, watch sports and take a break from work.

The IT industry is associated with a meritocratic ethos in direct contrast with the public sector where jobs and promotions are believed to be influenced either by official policies of positive discrimination (in favour of marginalized groups) or unofficial nepotistic tendencies. However, previous research on the profiles of IT workers indicates that recruitment tends to favour individuals with the right cultural capital to work closely with transnational clients (Upadhya and Vasavi, 2006; Krishna and Brihmadesam, 2006). Labelled 'soft skills', these cultural attributes include fluency in English, a cosmopolitan outlook, ability to mix freely with people outside of one's community and exposure to metropolitan lifestyles. As a result, a larger proportion of the IT workforce consists of employees who demonstrate these soft skills because they are educated in English medium rather than vernacular schools, from upper caste rather than lower caste families or from urban rather than rural backgrounds (Upadhya and Vasavi, 2006; Krishna and Brihmadesam, 2006; Upadhya, 2007), contradicting the industry's claim to egalitarianism and meritocracy (see public statements of the industry's leaders such as the NASSCOM blog post by Kiran Karnik, 2008).

The industry also claims to be strongly committed to recruiting and retaining women employees and providing them with a positive work environment through a number of policy initiatives, including recruitment targets, the option of extending the mandatory three months' maternity leave, company transport for those working late, day care for children and support for telecommuting by providing employees above a certain pay grade with Internet connectivity at home (Alexander, 2007; Nayare Ali, 2006; Ramalingam, 2007). The IT industry's pro-women image is celebrated in the press through articles with titles such as 'Women on Top!' (Alexander, 2007), 'IT's a Woman's World' (Ramalingam, 2007), 'India's New Worldly Women' (*Business Week*, 2005) and 'The Changing Indian Woman' (Bhagat, 2007). Subsequent chapters of the book will examine some ways in which these policies, particularly the option of telecommuting, actually impact individual women.

Bangalore: From pensioner's paradise to India's Silicon Valley

The self-image of the IT industry as a key player in India's integration into the global market has also influenced the image of the city where it originated: Bangalore has become synonymous with IT in India. However, it is a city of contrasts. Its many parks, lakes and wide tree-lined avenues are slowly disappearing; yet where they are still visible, one catches glimpses of the pensioners' paradise of the 1960s and the garden city of the 1970s and 1980s. The pubs, speciality restaurants, shopping malls, multiplexes, high-rise apartments and IT parks signal its metamorphosis into India's 'Silicon Valley' in the 21st century.

This is a Bangalore where the Internet cafes of the 1990s have already become redundant because their clientele access the Internet at home, at the office and in the car. Sociologist Thulasi Srinivas describes this 21st-century Bangalore: 'Young men and women with cell phones, laptops, and new cars are conspicuous. More than three hundred pubs in the central business district are packed on evenings and weekends with loud and noisy discussions of the latest change in management in Sunnyvale, Chicago or Bangalore' (Srinivas, 2002: 10). This is a Bangalore that the poor can only glimpse, a Bangalore that bewilders and dismays the city's older residents. But the young residents, members of the IT community, take pride in its globalized feel, as one of my interviewees suggests:

I was driving through the tech-park that is behind the Hewlett Packard office where the Dell and Microsoft offices are ... It was so good that it was a carbon copy of the Dubai Internet City – if you've ever seen a picture of that? [It was] ditto like that. That's when I felt let's forget the traffic, let's forget the infrastructure [problems] and everything, India's got that global feel. (Nitya, 27, manager, married)

While middle class IT workers can forget the traffic and infrastructural problems once they enter pristine confines of the technology park, the city's working classes and poor cannot. Nitya's remarks contrast sharply with those of an auto-rickshaw driver who was driving me through a traffic jam on Mahatma Gandhi Road (one of the busiest areas in Bangalore) during my fieldwork:

Look at the cars! They all get loans from their companies and they want to buy the biggest car possible. When the Tatas manufacture the one lakh car all these other people [pointing to the scooters and motorcycles] will want cars as well and there will be no space at all on the roads.[2] Garden City my foot! It's a *gaadi* [vehicle] city. (An auto-rickshaw driver in Bangalore speaking in Hindi)

Taken together these comments encapsulate the contradictions underlying the city's transformation and what that means in terms of quality of life, infrastructure and the polarization of classes. As the birthplace of the country's IT industry, Bangalore can be said to be a microcosm of globalization in India, mirroring the changes that are taking place in other metropolitan cities such as Chennai, Delhi and Mumbai. Like these cities it is becoming polarized on two levels: between the old and new middle classes who are represented by the older and newer residents of the city and between the poor and the 'new rich', represented by a section of the IT workers. Incidents of mugging IT professionals, of looting and of arson are often attributed to this polarization.

Bangalore has become a city of contrasts: glass-fronted buildings in landscaped gardens are flanked by slums and mud roads. The number of branded supermarkets has increased but the local greengrocer is ubiquitous. Old, established and highly respected missionary schools are in competition with new expensive private schools that boast Olympic-standard sports facilities and international curricula. There are several glaring infrastructural problems: traffic congestion, poorly maintained roads, poor waste disposal, overflowing public dustbins and shortage of electricity. I end this description of Bangalore with a quote from one of the participants in my research. Malini is currently taking a career break to look after her child. Perhaps this has given her a chance to reflect on the manner in which the new middle class in general and the IT industry in particular can insulate itself from the rest of the city in what she calls '*a beautiful world*' and '*a world with plenty*'.

> Your friends are in the same circle, your houses will be in the same circle, your thoughts are there twenty-four hours. You live in that world. It's a beautiful world and it's a world with plenty, but you have to be careful when you come back to reality. You travel in a lovely car, you have a driver or you have a [company] bus. He picks you, he drops you. Your food is taken care of. Everything is taken care of – door to office, office to door.

> Most of these guys, if you ask them what's happening in the world around them, they have no idea because they've been too busy having [taking] calls in the night. For twenty-four hours they're online. Except their codes and their jobs and their deliverables and their schedules, they don't know much. So their world, it's a very small world. Even when you go out of [the] country, you will find a friend of yours hanging around there. But what happens is you're not aware of the world outside. There are certain pockets where you have slums, they have problems, they have dacoities [robberies]. We have all kinds of issues. Probably you're not very careful about this because you're

secluded and you are comfortable in the world you've generated around you. (Malini, 33, currently not in employment (resigned as manager), mother)

Through this description of Bangalore and of the IT industry, I suggest that modernity has contradictory and complex consequences. It is neither uniform nor unilinear and, as I hope to show through the rest of this book, it is deeply gendered. However, these arguments in themselves are not new. This book takes these arguments further by suggesting that in contemporary post-industrial modernity (also called reflexive modernity or late modernity) where globalization seems to be creating a sense of uniformity across the world, experiences of modernity are culturally specific. It suggests, via qualitative research, that while neo-liberal ideologies and notions of individual reflexivity seem to enjoy high purchase across many parts of the world, this need not be taken as evidence of the triumph of individualization. Reflexivity is understood and experienced in culturally specific and gender-specific ways across the globe, one illustration of which is discussed in this book.

Organization of the book

In Chapter 2, I examine Giddens and Beck's reflexive modernity thesis, arguing for a fusion of the feminist critique of reflexivity with the broader sociological critique of modernity which comes from the Southern theory perspective. I suggest that to challenge the universalism implicit in the reflexive modernity thesis, we need to engage with empirical research that emerges from a Southern context. In Chapter 3, I attempt to locate middle class women in social and discursive terms by examining the challenges of defining the category 'middle class' in Indian society and the discursive production of Indian womanhood in contemporary India. In this manner I set up the context in which to examine middle class women's experiences in late modernity.

Chapters 4 to 7 form the ethnographic chapters of the book. Chapter 4 examines the manner in which research participants engage with traditional and contemporary discourses on women's positions in their families, introducing the argument that the individualism of Indian women is qualitatively different from individualism as understood by the reflexivity theorists. In Chapter 5, I examine women's motivations to work in the transnational economy and their relationships with paid work, while in Chapter 6 I consider some continuities and contradictions between paid employment and family life. In these chapters I suggest that women's engagement in paid labour is not an individualistic pursuit but is undertaken for the family. I argue that when families support their daughters and daughters-in-law in their professional life, they create relationships of mutual obligation which can both support and restrict women's participation in paid employment. Chapter 7 examines how women construct their sense of self within modernity and globalization, drawing on both traditional and contemporary discourses. I argue that decisions presented in the vocabulary of choice are often influenced by social, cultural and economic constraints and that the discourse of individual choice imposes greater responsibility on women for the consequences of choices which are not solely their own. I argue that seemingly opposed discourses sometimes reinforce each other.

I conclude by arguing that the Indian experience of contemporary modernity raises significant questions about the reflexive modernity thesis. I suggest that the notion of the individual project of self does not hold true in the case of middle class Indian women and argue for a new understanding of reflexivity based on the Indian context.

2
Interrogating Reflexive Modernity

Over the past twenty years a thesis has been gaining ground in sociology that globalization, the revolution of communication technologies and the widespread acceptance of neoliberal ideas have led to the growth of a society qualitatively different from anything the world has seen before. Changes in technology and communication are believed to be accompanied by transformations in several areas of social life, including intimacy, family life, childcare, the labour market and the workplace, and in individuals' subjective sense of self. These transformations are believed to be closely related with de-traditionalization, that is, the erosion of traditional ways of life and the valourization of the individual over the collective (whether that collective is the family, the trade union, the caste, the community, the church or the nation). De-traditionalization is believed to lead to the emancipation of women, the rise of a meritocratic social order where achievement is valued over ascriptive characteristics of birth and the rationalization of social life. Major proponents of this thesis of reflexive modernity (also called late modernity, second modernity or high modernity) include British sociologist Anthony Giddens (1990, 1991, 1992) and German sociologist Ulrich Beck who often works in collaboration with Elizabeth Beck-Gernsheim (1995, 2001). Zygmunt Bauman (2000, 2001) is also sometimes associated with this thesis, although there is some debate about whether the thrust of his ideas is closer to the postmodernists. In this book, I address the work of Beck and Giddens who not only are well established internationally but also are influential in their respective countries. Both theorists have done much to raise the profile of sociology outside of academia and contributed a great deal to the development of the discipline in the late 20th and early 21st centuries.

The question arises why interrogate the ideas of two sociologists whose theories proceed from a European context in a book about contemporary Indian, middle class women? One reason for doing so is the implied universalism of Giddens and Beck's theories and their assumption that modernity is a linear process. Another is that economic deregulation has created the conditions for the individualization of the labour market and strengthening of ideals such as individualism, autonomy and freedom. Therefore, it seems as if Indian society is developing along the lines described by the reflexivity theorists. In subsequent sections of this chapter I will further discuss why it is useful to examine the reflexive modernity thesis from the perspective of the Global South. At this stage, however, I draw attention to the manner in which popular discourse mirrors academic theory. Whilst I was working in Britain on the doctoral research that forms the basis of this book, my British colleagues would frequently compliment me on the 'strong family values' of my culture whilst bemoaning the erosion of family values in Britain. The system of arranging marriages often came up in conversation with senior colleagues joking that they would like to choose partners for their grown-up children. I would also be asked if the Indian joint family is disappearing due to globalization, the term 'globalization' being followed by another compliment, this time on India's 'booming economy'.

I tried to convince my colleagues that Indian families do disagree from time to time, that not all Indians consent to arranged marriages and that many who do often have the casting vote when it comes to choosing a spouse. Yes, globalization seems to be creating change but its consequences are varied and not easy to grasp. Moreover, I would add, that India is a country of over one billion people, many of whom have been increasingly marginalized by India's neoliberal economic reforms. I usually ended such conversations by assuring my listeners that what I had just told them about Indian families and women's positions in them was at best a generalization. Given the diversity of castes, classes and religious groups within Indian society, I would add, the opposite of what I had said may also be argued. My remarks possibly left them somewhat bewildered and annoyed at my fickleness.

In response to enquiries in India about 'the self-centred and mechanical life' in the West, I usually responded that I did not feel equipped to comment on British culture based on my short experience of the country but that the people I met do make time for their families. I had seen parents supporting their children and children taking care of ageing parents. What intrigued me, however, were the parallels between popular and academic discourses on modernity. I also noted, with some amusement, that the belief that society is undergoing a transformation wherein tradition is steadily eroded by individual choice and freedom seems to be cherished across cultures.

However, while I was away, other, more serious issues cropped up in and around the city I called home. The state of Karnataka has generally been accepting diverse cultural values for much of the 20th century. Over the last few years, however, right-wing political parties have become increasingly popular in the state. These parties support a fairly traditional and circumscribed role for women, violently opposing what they deem as the degradation of Indian traditions by the adoption of 'liberated Western practices' (Valentine's Day celebrations for instance). Mangalore, a coastal city of Karnataka, some 350 kilometres from Bangalore, has seen violent attacks under the label of 'cultural policing' on men and women drinking together in pubs or socializing at parties. Such incidents indicate the danger inherent in monochromatic views of modernity. While sociologists of modernity may not intend for their theses to be used in favour of extremism, and while perpetrators of violence may not necessarily be conversant with the theories of Giddens and Beck, I would argue that somewhat straightforward theoretical associations of modernity with de-traditionalization and women's emancipation mask the ways in which traditions continue to remain influential and disguise the complexity of women's relationship with modernity.

In Chapter 3, I discuss how women are often implicated in discourses about modernity and anxieties about the erosion of tradition. In this chapter I examine two valuable critiques of the reflexive modernity thesis: one derived from a macro-sociological perspective and the other from feminism. In the first part of this chapter I briefly summarize the main tenets of the reflexive modernity thesis. While this summary is not exhaustive, an attempt is made to give the readers from other disciplinary backgrounds a sense of the general thrust of the modernity thesis and discuss those aspects of Beck's and Giddens' theories that are relevant to this book: the notion of the self as a reflexive project and the consequences of individualization for women. Readers who are familiar with Giddens' and Beck's ideas may choose to skip this section and move directly to the critiques of the reflexivity thesis. Finally I consider some alternatives to the notion of extended reflexivity, noting elements of these alternative theoretical perspectives that would be useful in subsequent chapters. I end by arguing that a fusion of the Southern theory perspective with the feminist perspective creates a powerful critique of reflexivity which forms the basis of this book.

The reflexive modernity thesis

Rationalization and risk

The primary contention of the reflexive modernity theorists is that modernity underwent a transformational shift in the late 20th century so that it is fundamentally different from Enlightenment modernity. At the same time they are emphatic that we have not entered a postmodern era. Unlike the postmodernists who tend to view the current period as one of de-centralization and fragmentation, Giddens and Beck see it in terms of universalizing tendencies: the interdependence of national economies through globalization, widespread de-traditionalization as a result of cultural change, the magnification of risk on a regional and global scale and the growth of institutionalized individualism. This shift has led to what has been variously termed 'second modernity', 'reflexive modernity', 'late modernity' and 'high modernity'. For the reflexive modernists, modernity has not ended; it has merely intensified to a point where it looks and feels different from earlier forms of modernity. While Beck and Giddens may emphasize different aspects of this shift, two recurrent themes occur in both their theories: rationalization and risk.

Giddens (1990) sees the expansion of modernity as a result of the penetration of the nation state model, capitalism, industrialism and the means of territorial surveillance, that is, the rationalization of political and economic life. He succinctly describes this historical turn in terms of three major processes: the separation of time and space, the disembedding of social relationships 'from local contexts of interaction and their restructuring across infinite expanses of time-space' and institutional reflexivity (Giddens, 1990: 21, 1991). The separation of space and time refers to the forging of social relationships across geographical areas, which are enabled by the standardization of time zones. Improvement in the technology of communication enables 'the precise coordination of the actions of many human beings physically absent from one another: the "when" of these actions is directly connected to the "where" but not, as in pre-modern epochs, via the mediation of place' (Giddens, 1991: 17).

The disembedding of social relations is a result of two kinds of mechanisms: abstract tokens and expert systems or the rationalization of global financial systems and knowledge. A typical example of an abstract token is money which enables transactions between actors who are not in physical contact with one another. Expert systems refer to the technological expertise of professionals such as doctors, lawyers, counsellors, scientists and engineers who create the systems through which we organize our daily lives. Giddens argues that, within late modernity, knowledge about social life begins to inform social life. Institutional reflexivity is the result of human knowledge and ideas becoming the means by which human beings assess their actions and organize social life. However, reflexivity also suggests that knowledge is only credible until proven otherwise. Thus late modernity creates conditions for undermining rational thought and expert knowledge such as psychology, medicine and law even as they become the basis for social action.

Although Giddens (1991) acknowledges the existence of risk in this period of modernity, which he argues creates the need for ontological security amongst members of society, it is Beck (1999) who may be credited with theorizing the collective recognition of risks. As the world comes to grips with national and global risks such as HIV/AIDS, SARS, global warming and climate change, a sense of shared responsibility emerges. The risk becomes everybody's problem and solutions require everybody's participation. Complex negotiations are carried out to determine how the fallout of the risk should be shared. To Beck (1999) reflexivity connotes the reflexive reactions towards risks and uncertainty. In this book I consider the consequences of late modernity and globalization in work and personal life; therefore, it is those aspects of Giddens' and Beck's theories that are relevant here. However, the notion of contingency and contradiction are the backdrop against which individuals' personal and working lives are played out.

Individualization

Giddens may be credited with creating a space for individual agency within sociological analysis via his theory of self-identity. Rather than seeing individuals as victims of the structural conditions of their existence, he suggests that they might creatively engage with social structure in order to make room for personal needs or express subjective desires. His emphasis on individual agency can be said to counter both the pessimism of post-structuralism and postmodernism, and the overt determinism of earlier structural functionalist, Marxist and Bourdieusian social theory. The structuralist self is determined by structural and material privileges and disprivileges while the post-structuralist self is disciplined by powerful discourses over which it has little or no influence. In contrast the postmodernist self is fragmented and illusionary, always in the process of becoming, never finished. Giddens' self, although a work in progress, is not overburdened by structural constraints or regulated by cultural forces. Instead it is self-reflexive and self-referential. Though in a constant process of becoming, at any given moment it can look back on itself and construct a coherent biography. However, Giddens does not examine how this might work on a daily basis, leaving to others the work of investigating empirically how a reflexive biography is constructed.

While other theories of globalization tended to examine broader issues such as world capitalism (Wallerstein, 2004) or the flow of ideas and culture across national borders (Appadurai, 1996), Giddens and Beck bring the individual into the analysis of globalization. While they acknowledge the role of deepening capitalism, development of media and communication technologies and the replication of the nation state model across the globe, their analysis focuses on the implications of these processes for individuals' sense of self, family life and intimate relationships. Both theorists view globalization as closely implicated with de-traditionalization and individualization, but as Heaphy (2007) argues, Beck's work is more concerned with the tensions and contingencies produced by globalization while Giddens' is engaged with the possibilities for reconstituting personal, social and political lives.

Giddens (1990, 1991, 1999) suggests that globalization is more likely to destabilize traditional identities and ways of life by bringing individuals into contact with cultures that are significantly different from their own. In his 1999 treatise, *Globalization in a Runaway World*, Giddens begins by arguing, via Hobsbawm, that tradition is itself a construct of modernity, that traditions are invented and reinvented over time, that they travel across time and space via communication technologies and that local identities become stronger in response to globalization. However, he goes on to state that 'there cannot but be a large dollop of rationality in the persistence of religious rituals and observances in a de-traditionalising society. And this is exactly as it should be' (Giddens, 2002: 45). Thus he not only seems to contradict his earlier suggestion that tradition is a by-product of modernity by not only conflating modernity with de-traditionalization but also quite clearly endorsing this characteristic of modernizing (Western) societies.

The idea of the self as an individual project is the foundation of Giddens' theory of self-identity. For Giddens globalization and de-traditionalization have given rise to a world where familiar injunctions of state, religion, family and community regarding who one is and how one should live are steadily eroded. Individuals are in a position to question taken-for-granted collective identities of family, community, religion or state and begin re-fashioning a personal identity that draws from a variety of identity choices: choices 'not only how to act but who to be' (Giddens, 1991: 81). The self as a reflexive project, Giddens

argues, is late modernity's answer to the individual's need for ontological security in a world of myriad choice and multiple risks where
the religious and spiritual explanations for and antidotes to risk have
been considerably undermined. As individuals are increasingly thrown
on their own resources and expected to make decisions and choices
regarding work, family relationships, education, sexual orientation and
lifestyle, as they calibrate risk or examine possibilities, 'the self becomes
a *reflexive project*', created and sustained by human action and decision
(Giddens, 1991: 32, emphasis in original).

Giddens argues that lifestyle choices and life planning 'form the institutional settings which help to shape individual actions and are a universal
feature of individuals' lives in late-modernity *irrespective of privilege or dis-
privilege, economic or social circumstances*' (Giddens, 1991: 85, emphasis
mine). As the individual reflects on decisions and plans for the future,
she creates a coherent biographical narrative which is necessary for psychological well-being. 'Self-identity is not a distinctive trait, or even a
collection of traits possessed by the individual. It is the *self as reflexively
understood by the person in terms of her or his biography*' (Giddens, 1991:
53, emphasis in original).

Giddens' late-modern individual, with her capacity for reflexively constructing a self-identity through a narrative understanding of the past
and plans for the future, may be viewed as an antithesis of Foucault's
(1976/1990) self-monitoring individual whose self is shaped by powerful
cultural discourses over which she has little or no influence. Foucault's
individual is subjected to the control of powerful forces external to herself which inscribe on her a selfhood through knowledge(s) of the body
and mind. As the individual internalizes this knowledge, the mechanisms of control and discipline are also internalized as self-discipline.
Through his examination of medical and psychological discourses and
discursive practices, Foucault argues that they reveal to the individual
an embodied selfhood wherein even self-examination or self-knowledge
becomes a strategy for disciplining the self. As opposed to Focualt's
disciplined self, Giddens' (1991) self is highly empowered and liberated
from the constraints of traditional structures. In the pursuit of self-
actualization, this self assesses opportunities and risks, making choices
that increase her sense of self-worth and underline her authenticity (the
idea of a 'true self' as distinguished from a false one). This is a highly
positive view of individualization, one in which the tensions, contradictions and dilemmas that the individual faces have little place.

In contrast, Beck views the eroding influence of traditional identity
markers such as religion and culture and modern identities such as class

with more concern. He suggests that institutionalized individualism creates a paradoxical situation wherein individuals are expected to plan their life-courses, making decisions based on a careful consideration of risks and possibilities, yet they are seldom in a position to influence the conditions in which they create their biographies. Since traditions have lost their reified status in late modern society, they have to be chosen and defended by individuals who attempt to define themselves through the traditions that they uphold.

Beck and Beck-Gernsheim view globalization as a key factor in individualization, bringing together as it does diverse cultures and traditions, and challenging individuals to negotiate between conflicting identities and traditions. Moreover, it changes both the nature and the scale of risks and uncertainties that individuals encounter whilst destabilizing the traditional structures which enabled individuals to face the uncertainties of life. 'If globalization, de-traditionalization and individualization are analysed together', they argue, 'it becomes clear that the life of own is an experimental life. Inherited recipes for living and role stereotypes fail to function. There are no historical models for the conduct of life. Individual and social life – in marriage and parenthood as well as in politics, public activity and paid work – have to be brought back into harmony with each other' (Beck and Beck-Gernsheim, 2001: 26).

Beck and Beck-Gernsheim's analysis makes it possible to consider the challenges of de-traditionalization, individualization and free choice. Individualism is accompanied by decrease in job security, the rollback of the welfare state and the growth of a neoliberal market economy. At the same time, planning of one's life-course and the construction of one's self-identity are a cultural imperative and an individual responsibility. Individualization becomes fate rather than choice (Bauman, 2000: 34) as individual members of society seek 'biographical solutions to systemic contradictions' (Beck, 1992: 137 in Bauman, 2000: 34) rather than work collectively for social change.

The consequences of individualization for women

As with individualization in general, Giddens and Beck have divergent notions of its consequences for women. Taking an optimistic view, Giddens argues that freeing sexuality from traditional norms and controls has resulted in the trend towards forging 'pure relationships', that is, relationships sought with a view to what they 'can bring to the partners involved' (Giddens, 1991: 90). As sexuality is de-linked from reproduction, individuals are no longer bound together for life. Instead they choose to remain in a relationship for the length of time that they receive emotional and psychological benefit from it (Giddens, 1992). Although Giddens (1992) acknowledges that men often have contradictory expectations of women, wanting a partner who is intellectually and economically equal yet expecting traditionalism in devotion to family and children, he argues that the democratization of family life and marital relationships can potentially free women from oppressive and exploitative relationships.

In comparison Beck and Beck-Gernsheim (2001) take a somewhat pessimistic view of the family in late modernity. They argue that individualization creates a stress on family life due to the 'contradictions between family demands and personal freedom' (Beck and Beck-Gernsheim, 1995: 2). Two individuals both engaged in creating their biographies through personal and professional achievements may find that their life-plans often contradict each other, a contradiction that is exacerbated by the conflicting demands of the labour market and family life.

Keen observers of the contradictions in contemporary modernity, they argue that the workplace requires flexibility, mobility and aggressive competitiveness while family life is dependent on stability, rootedness and concern for others (Beck-Gernsheim, 2002). In the labour market, the worker is seen as a 'flexible work unit, competitive and ambitious, prepared to disregard the social commitments linked to his/her existence and identity ... prepared to move whenever necessary' (Beck and Beck-Gernsheim, 1995: 6). This was possible when one member in the relationship devoted herself to the home, but in a situation where both partners are equally devoted to their professional commitments, a high degree of stress enters the relationship. In negotiating the multiple contradictions of their social realities and their own expectations from each other, partners carry out complex negotiations before and during the marriage. They attempt to match their individual aims and plans with that of the other person. An inability to match individual biographies can cause marital or relationship breakdown (Beck and Beck-Gernsheim, 1995).

The contradictions between the labour market and families are mirrored in women's internal struggle between living for others and living a life of one's own, between taking on the major responsibility for family tasks and their 'expectations and wishes that extend beyond the family' (Beck and Beck-Gernsheim, 2001: 67). While they have more opportunities for paid employment, inequalities continue to persist in the labour market which result in low-pay, short-term contracts and job insecurity, which might cause a (mostly involuntary) retreat into family life.

To summarize, the reflexive modernity thesis implies that all societies across the globe are moving, albeit at different speeds, towards a more rationalized, egalitarian and democratic order. Within such an order the individual is respected and emancipated from the constraints of race, ethnicity, class and gender. Individual achievement and dignity are valued over birth and lineage. Life choices are no longer constrained by conditions of birth, and we are free to create our identities from the diverse options that society affords us. Those who have been marginalized over the course of history finally have a chance at empowerment. There is equality or at least the expectation of equality between the sexes. While we might face conflicts and contradictions between the 'no longer' and 'not yet' of our march towards equality (Beck and Beck-Gernsheim, 2001: 55–56), for both men and women there is no turning back.

This post-traditional social order with its emphasis on rationality and egalitarianism is believed to be embodied by the economically established societies of the North and is seen as the future of the southern hemisphere. Perhaps the reason for the popularity of the reflexivity thesis is that it seems to explain the much talked of pockets of affluence in India, China and other Asian societies. Cities such as Bangalore, Singapore, Shanghai and Kuala Lumpur become early examples of the march towards reflexive modernity. Their culture is seen to be open and welcoming of individualism, difference and diversity. Their middle classes are believed to conform to the notions of individualization described in Giddens' and Beck's theories. They are able to create a reflexive self based on personal choice and are less constrained by the dictates of religion or tradition than their parents might have been. Their involvement in economic, social and cultural exchange with the Global North indicates the influence of globalization on their daily lives. Thus Asia, Africa and South America are believed to follow Europe in the march towards modernity not because of political or economic constraints but because 'modernity is so irresistible' (Connell, 2008).

The reflexive modernity suggests neither the degradation of non-European societies nor their marginalization, but welcomes them into modernity, extending to them the blessings of democracy, free-market capitalism and rationality. Therefore it is unapologetic about the possible erosion of local cultures and traditions along the way. 'Is modernity a distinctively Western project in terms of the ways of life fostered by these two great transformative agencies [the nation state and systematic capitalist production]? To this query, the blunt answer must be "yes"' (Giddens, 1990: 174–175).

Critiques of the reflexive modernity thesis

Critiques of the reflexive modernity thesis have emerged from two are-nas: from contemporary sociologists of modernity and from sociologists of the self whose work overlaps with the feminist tradition. The former take a macro-sociological perspective, arguing against broad assumptions of modernity theories in conceptual terms. The latter emerge largely, though not exclusively, from empirical research undertaken in a European context on women and family life. Though there are over-laps between the two, it may be argued that the former is more focused on the Eurocentricism inherent in modernity theories while the latter questions its masculinist assumptions. Therefore both critiques comple-ment each other.

The macro-sociological critique

The contemporary sociological critique of modernity is not just con-cerned with questioning Giddens and Beck but with interrogating a number of assumptions of modernity theorists. It suggests that in spite of their assertion that contemporary modernity is different from the first modernity that followed Enlightenment, Giddens and Beck are continuing the Enlightenment legacy by taking a broad-brush view of the world. The Enlightenment thinkers and sociologists of the 19th century tended to generalize from the European experience, overlook-ing both colonialism and the unique trajectories of change inside and outside Europe. When experiences of 'Other' cultures were consid-ered, it was usually to justify a continuum of evolution that ended in European modernity. Whilst the end of colonialism and the rise of postcolonial academies of thought have made it impossible to ignore the diversity of experiences across the world, portions of contemporary social theory, including the reflexivity thesis, tend to be created without adequate reference to the specific experiences of postcolonial societies. By highlighting some Eurocentric biases within the reflexive modernity thesis, the contemporary critique of modernity lays the foundation for constructing what Raewyn Connell (2008) might term 'a Southern theory of modernity'.

It has been argued that by positioning reflexive modernity as post-traditional modernity, the reflexivity thesis obscures the significance of tradition in the contemporary period (King, 1999). Since Hobsbawm's (1983) treatise on the subject, sociologists have recognized that tradi-tions are invented within specific social and historical conditions and often to create distinct national or ethnic identities. Giddens (2002) acknowledges that traditions are invented and reinvented over time and that modernity enables them to travel beyond local contexts via communication technologies. He also contends that local identities become stronger in response to globalization. However he also believes that by enabling encounters between diverse traditions, globalization creates conditions for traditions to become increasingly destabilized. By equating de-traditionalization with contemporary modernity, Giddens implies that traditions have been accepted unquestioningly before modernity.

As Paul Heelas (1996) argues, individual desires and traditions are often in conflict, so it is not to be supposed that contemporary societies are more pluralistic than the so-called traditional societies. Traditions upheld by different groups in society may vary considerably; in cases of conflict between traditions those of dominant groups usually prevail. John Thompson (1996) suggests that while tradition may have lost its relevance as a means to 'make sense of the world' and provide legitimacy for certain forms of authority, it continues to play a role in defining individual and collective identities. Within modernity traditions become a means to define symbolic and actual boundaries between groups. By re-enacting traditions or recreating them through digital, print and other media, migrants and diasporas create a sense of belonging with their homeland and claim a distinct identity in their host communities. He suggests that while 'traditions are less sheltered than ever before from the potentially invigorating consequences of encounters with the other', contemporary modernity cannot be considered post-traditional society (Thompson, 1996: 106). Thompson (1996) offers a more nuanced way of looking at tradition, understanding it in terms of diverse identities, beliefs and practices, some of which continue to be relevant.

Connell argues that Giddens proceeds as if the modernity of the rest of the world simply follows that of Europe. In other words European domination is attributed to its 'temporal precedence' and not to the violence of colonialism (Connell, 2008: 38). She contents that in addition to this false universalism, much of Northern theory (using the UN's terminological classification of the world into North and South) tends to read from the centre and erase the experiences of large parts of the world. Gurminder Bhambra makes a similar critique of Beck's notion of cosmopolitan sociology, arguing that instead of calling for enabling different voices to be heard in the face of globalization, Beck needs to recognize that a truly cosmopolitan sociology needs to provincialize European understandings of the world (Holmwood, 2007 in Bhambra, 2009). The Enlightenment paradigm positions modernity as a universalizing project. It fails to recognize the cultural specificities of different modernizing societies.

The reflexive modernity thesis does not examine the relationship between colonialism and modernity. As Bhambra (2009) and Connell (2008) argue, it is important to recognize that for much of the early modern period, colonialism and imperialism created the conditions within which cultures encountered each other, conditions which when not violent were certainly unequal. The lenses of Orientalism and primitiveness through which Europeans viewed colonized cultures continue to influence both popular and academic perspectives in Europe. Moreover, experiences of colonialism also colour the way in which many postcolonial cultures view Europe and the relationship that they have with modernity. As Ashis Nandy (1983: 63) evocatively argued 30 years ago, 'colonialism is first of all a matter of consciousness', a collective ideology in the minds of the colonizer and the colonized wherein Europe is constructed as the adult masculine self and Asia and Africa as its childlike, feminine-untutored Other, to be regulated accordingly.

For nations which have been otherized in European thought, aspirations for modernity are irrevocably bound with colonialism and imperialism (Bhambra, 2009; Connell, 2008). Modernity for them is not a space of universality and uniformity but a space which is marked by the contradictions of culture, history and power. The modernity of these nations is not identical to a universal 'European' model (if Europe may be taken for argument's sake as a monolithic entity). To represent it as a series of 'modernities' which share certain common characteristics whilst having some culturally specific differences would be useful but not enough. Bhambra (2009) argues that to understand modernity, we need to move beyond discourses of multiple or alternative modernities, which continue to position European modernity as 'original'. Even postcolonial perspectives, she argues, question existing paradigms of knowledge but without challenging the categories of the colonizer and the colonized through which these paradigms are constructed. Cultural relativism also fails to offer a concrete solution since it does not recognize the connections and overlaps between cultures. She argues for understanding the fragile threads that connect European modernity to that of different parts of the globe and their mutual influence on each other. The modernity of non-European nations is constituted within specific histories of colonialism and unequal power relations, which continue to mark globalization (Bhambra, 2009).

Bhambra's and Nandy's arguments are particularly important to discussions about gender and modernity. Experiences of colonialism and imperialism had specific implications for constructions of masculinity and femininity in the cultures of the colonizers and the colonized. Within postcolonial nations women's relationship with modernity is often the subject of heated debate. While women's positions may be viewed as indicators of modernity, they also become representatives of the nation's traditions. Therefore any discussion of changing gender identities or changing gender relations within modernity or reflexive modernity needs to take into account experiences of colonialism. In Chapter 3, I explore in detail how nationalist debates on 'the women's question' continue to influence contemporary understandings of Indian womanhood.

The macro-sociological critique of modernity enables us to re-think some core paradigms of modernity and creates the conditions for developing a Southern theory of modernity, which if strengthened by empirical work could lead to a more nuanced understanding of modernity than the reflexivity thesis suggests. It also offers a way to examine the complexities in the relationship between modernity and tradition. It interrogates the meta-narratives of unidirectionality, rationalization and standardization. However, it does not consider, in depth, those sections of the reflexive modernity thesis that relate to personal life. Since family life, gender relations and selfhood tend to be the sites where the contradictions of modernity are played out, a deeper understanding of these issues requires us to turn to feminist critiques of modernity.

The feminist critique

Feminists have argued that Giddens and Beck seem to have overstated individual agency within reflexive modernity and overlooked the role of power in shaping individual subjectivity (Adkins, 2000; Smart and Shipman, 2004; Jackson, 2008; Mulinari and Sandell, 2009). This, they argue, has led reflexive modernity theorists to exaggerate the capacity of individualization to improve the status of women. They claim that Giddens undermines the importance of resources for shaping a reflexive narrative of self. The self is not as coherent as Giddens suggests but complex and contextual. It is much more constrained by structural inequalities and cultural factors than Giddens seems to imply. Access to these resources are based on structural differences of class, ethnicity, race and gender (Adkins, 2000; Skeggs, 2004; Heaphy, 2007; Smart, 2007; Adams, 2003). For instance, given their nurturing responsibilities and identification with the work of care, women's subjective sense of self may not be as individualized as Giddens suggests. Based on Lash and Urry's concept of reflexivity's winners and losers, Adkins (2000) suggests that women often end up as reflexivity's losers whilst empowering men to become reflexivity's winners. However, I would argue that winning and losing are not water-tight categories but points on a continuum where individuals are positioned based on the intersections of gender, class, ethnicity and geography.

Giddens has also been criticized for tending to universalize a White, middle class, masculine notion of reflexivity and failing to account for the unequal access that different individuals have to the resources for creating a self-identity based on class, gender, race ethnicity and occupation (Skeggs, 2004; Adkins, 2000; Adams, 2003, 2006; Jamieson, 1999; Mulinari and Sandell, 2009). Based on their examination of transnational identities in Britain, Smart and Shipman (2004) argue that Giddens does not recognize that choices are contextualized and mediated by culture. Within their cultural circumstances, and based on differences of class, gender, race or ethnicity, individuals have access to different types of choices. By presenting individualization and choice in universalistic terms, Giddens and Beck tend to marginalize difference in access to choice. Not only are choices limited by structural factors and cultural identities, but they are also not necessarily always liberating (Adams, 2006 via Bauman, 1998; Smart and Shipman, 2004). For instance, in their interviews with Asian women in Britain regarding questions of identity and choice, Smart and Shipman (2004: 19) found that they were confronted with difficult choices between allegiance to their communities and personal freedom or between doing what was best for their children and for themselves – their choices then become 'Hobson's choices' between injustice to themselves or to others.

The concept of 'choice' may often be used to rationalize gendered decisions regarding the division of labour in the household, women's withdrawal from the labour market or the prioritization of men's careers over those of women's as the following chapters will argue. By positioning these decisions as choices based on personal life-plans or mutual affection, individuals tend to mask the inequalities in the labour market and in heterosexual relationships that influence these choices (Williams, 2000). A key argument of this book is that the notion of individual choice is part of a discourse that exerts pressure on individuals (women) to take responsibility for their own well-being whilst masking structural factors that limit individual freedom.

Giddens' theory of self-identity fails to account for 'the complexity of selfhood' and 'ignores the potential messiness of self-identity' (Heaphy, 2007: 102, quoting Lash, 1993). In their daily lives individuals may confront conflicting identities to which they feel allegiance. However,

Giddens' individuals rarely experience self-doubt and never seem to feel torn apart between identities. They confidently choose or discard identities in a bid to create a coherent narrative of self.

While Beck and Beck-Gernsheim seem to have a better grasp on the contradictions and challenges of individualization for women, they have been criticized for ignoring the continuities between gender inequalities in the public and private sphere (Mulinari and Sandell, 2009). Inequalities between men and women in the labour market could influence family life just as the sexual division of labour in the family can have an impact on the individual's chances in the labour market. While they suggest that women are often caught between the demands of public roles and family life, they do not examine the ways in which women might address this conflict.

In a critique of Beck-Gernsheim's discussion of families in late modernity, Smart argues that she seems to proceed as if 'all the previous debates on changes in the family never happened' (Smart, 2007: 18). The discussion tends to take an apocalyptic nature as assertions about the disappearance of 'the family as we know it' are made, raising questions about whose family is under discussion and who the 'we' being referred to might be. Previous debates on changes in family life have taken similar sweeping perspectives where the nuclear family was considered the new family formation that replaced the (already, always existing) extended family (Smart, 2007). If indeed the nuclear family is becoming extinct what is it being replaced by? On this matter Beck and Beck-Gernsheim remain silent.

Both Giddens and Beck tend to take as 'natural' heterosexual nuclear families (Mulinari and Sandell, 2009) rather than viewing them as *one* outcome of specific social, cultural and economic circumstances. The variety of family formations that are increasingly evident in late modernity – whether in the Global North or in the South, including same-sex couples, reconstitute families, step families, single-parent families, families consisting of two to three generations of women and their children and the intergenerational families (households) – find no place in their analysis. The naturalization and normalization of the heterosexual nuclear family (preferably with two children: a boy and a girl) was for much of the 1970s and 1980s the message of the state-sponsored family-planning propaganda in India. Such a message is dangerous because it tends to position as deviant all other family formations, exposing its members to ridicule, ostracism and perhaps even violence (for instance, communities that do not support contraception are not represented in this type of discourse). Moreover, the failure to distinguish between families and households makes it even more problematic to understand continuities and changes in the institution as I discuss in Chapter 4.

Giddens in particular takes an idealized view of families, particularly of relationships between spouses. While one may agree with Smart (2007), that implicit in his discussion is the notion that the weaker members of the family should be treated fairly, it is this 'should' that moves his argument from the realm of the theoretical to the polemical; that is, his description seems to fit an ideal that is widely prevalent in our culture rather than an empirical reality. Examining women's accounts of their family relationships, in Chapter 4, I argue along with Jamieson (1999) that the value placed on democracy in intimate relations results in couples attempting to engage resources to conceal the unequal and undemocratic aspects of their relationships or constructing narratives to justify them. Giddens confines himself to discussing the emotive and sexual aspects of relationships, not taking into account issues such as the sexual division of labour and the structural inequalities in families. Economic, social and cultural imperatives that might stand in the way of individuals leaving a couple relationship when it ceases to fulfil their needs find no mention in his argument.

While Beck and Beck-Gernsheim analyse more closely than Giddens the unequal responsibility that women have for care work, they do not recognize inequalities between women in terms of the global care chain and the capacity of some women to buy themselves out of care at the expense of others (Mulinari and Sandell, 2009). European feminists have argued that their discussion of the labour market inequalities that women face does not consider intersectionalities of race and class which can further complicate gender discrimination (Mulinari and Sandell, 2009). From a Southern feminist perspective, it may also be said that they fail to account for the intergenerational exchange of care between women, a major factor in women's labour-market participation in India (and possibly other parts of the world). As empirical chapters of this book will indicate, these intergenerational obligations are key in influencing not only women's relationships with paid employment but also their sense of self. However, they find no place in the reflexivity thesis.

While the feminist critique is valuable in underscoring the masculinist assumptions inherent in the reflexivity thesis, till recently it has come mainly from within European contexts. However, more recently a few critiques of individualization have arisen from the Global South, for instance, Jackson's (2008) discussion of gender and sexuality in East

Asia and Chang and Song's (2010) examination of individualization in South Korea. Jackson argues that lesbian women's experiences of negotiating the marginalization and stigmatization of homosexuality in East Asia suggest that 'reflexivity can operate under conditions of choice *and* constraint' (Jackson, 2008: 63, emphasis in original). Examining women's experiences of modernity in South Korea, Chang and Song argue that the increasing age of marriage, falling fertility rates and increasing number of 'covert divorces' (which are outside official records) suggest that South Korean women are becoming individualized, but at the level of ideas they do not support individualism. They continue to be fairly family-centred although there are intergenerational differences between them. Jackson's and Song and Chang's work suggests that individualization and its effect on family life need to be understood in a culturally specific context, thereby challenging the implied universalism in Giddens' work.

The aspiration towards modernity and the desire to reinforce tradition in many Southern cultures have unique consequences for women. The expansion of the free-market economy to emerging economies of the Global South, the penetration of consumerist tendencies and the popularity of neoliberal ideologies have created the conditions for culturally distinctive and gendered modernities to develop across the Global South. The next few chapters further develop the feminist critique of the reflexivity thesis by examining it in the light of empirical evidence from India. Before moving on to these, however, I consider some alternative perspectives on reflexivity.

Alternative notions of reflexivity

Given the gaps in the reflexivity thesis discussed above, I examine below three alternative notions of reflexivity: Scott Lash's alternative based on postmodern and post-structuralist theorists, Bauman and Foucault, respectively; Mathew Adam's alternative based on the Bourdieusian idea of habitus, and Stevi Jackson's alternative based on the theories of George Herbert Mead.

Lash: Reflexivity as discourse

Lash (1993) argues that the reflexivity thesis cannot address questions of contingency and power, for which we need to turn to theorists such as Bauman and Foucault. He argues that while Beck and Giddens focus on risk, Bauman focuses on contingency. Giddens and Beck seem to view reflexivity as a means of calculating risk, whereas Bauman views the contemporary individual as always engaged with contingency (Lash, 1993), never able to commit fully to a given identity, course of action or way of life. All decisions and commitments are only made until further notice. By focusing on contingency, Bauman takes a much more pessimistic view of the contemporary individual.

Giddens' expert systems, Lash goes on to argue, are similar to Foucault's discourses which 'govern, individualize and normalize subjects' (1993: 20). However, while expert systems may impose some order on the chaos of choice and support individuals in making choices, discourses act as powerful influencers of individual action. While power is no longer exercised by direct control of the body, discourses of late modernity enable a mediated control over the body via the soul. Thus the freedom of agency that the theory of reflexivity celebrates becomes a tool of capitalist production, for instance, in the form of entrepreneurship, and the discourse a means of influencing the individual's reflexivity. Extending this argument, it may be suggested that freedom to choose may be viewed itself as a discourse of late modernity.

The Foucauldian idea of discourse is useful in understanding the popularity of the notion of individual choice and responsibility in the contemporary period. The notion of individualism is strengthened by the words of experts (psychologists, counselors, self-help books, media and advertising) and the education system which rewards individual effort and achievement. The state relies on this discourse to roll back on welfare and support in key sectors such as education, employment and care. In the labour market, the individual is encouraged to take responsibility for her own professional success by seeking work and training opportunities that enhance her employability, by taking calculated risks and by keeping sight of potential opportunities. From the industrial to the post-industrial period, employers are less responsible for their employees' career success and financial stability. Employees on their part are not expected to maintain lifelong loyalty to one employer or manager, but to develop 'portfolio careers' by seeking a variety of professional experiences. In an environment where jobs are regularly under threat and where the global economy is perceived to be vulnerable to risk and uncertainty, the discourse of individual choice and responsibility enjoys high purchase. It enables employers and the state to abdicate to individuals the responsibility for their own welfare while giving them a wider range of options.

However, even while we accept that individual choice and responsibility are a discourse, we need to be aware of the implications of this argument. Discourses, as Foucault sees them, leave little scope for individual agency. Foucault's individual is almost involuntarily and unilaterally influenced by discourse. Even his later work on the technologies of the self does not allow much room for individuals to actively engage with discursive forces accepting, discarding or making sense of the discourse for themselves. Moreover, there is little space for discussion of competing discourses in his analysis.

In this book I view discourses not as fixed entities but as malleable and adaptable. Discourses change under the influence of individual agency. Individuals engage elements of a discourse to create their self-identities rather than being unilaterally subjected to their coercive influence. By engaging elements of one discourse rather than another, individuals might be able to creatively negotiate the influence of discourses. The extent to which an individual might be able to do so depends on the intersections of class, ethnicity, race and gender, but all individuals have some capacity to strategically engage with discourses. While accepting Lash's criticisms of reflexivity from a Foucauldian perspective, it is important to resist Foucault's deterministic view of the influence of discourses. With this view, I now turn to other alternatives to Giddens' ideas.

Adams: The darker sides of reflexivity

In an ambitious project that attempts to hybridize the Bourdieusian concept of habitus with Giddens' reflexivity, Adams (2006) argues that it is important to avoid oscillating between the determinism of one and the voluntarism of the other. Reflexivity implies the existence of a weak social structure and an individual who is relatively free, flexible and emancipated. On the other hand Bourdieu suggests that the social structure is relatively fixed for individual social groups and that individuals learn the habitual ways in which to engage with the social structure within their groups. There is something involuntary and unconscious about the manner in which individuals learn and deploy these habitual dispositions. Within this theory even reflexivity could be seen as an acquired disposition rather than an autonomous process or a questioning of given ways of being. Examining a range of theories that employ Bourdieu's analysis, Adams argues that women may be able to challenge, resist or negotiate with structural constraints but within delimited boundaries. He draws on Skeggs and McNay to argue that 'reflexivity is a creative possibility, but it is founded on pre-reflexive commitments originating in the social world which shape that possibility' (Adams, 2006: 517).

Adams argues that while all social groups may have some degree of reflexivity, they might not all have access to forms of reflexivity that are transformative and emancipatory. He suggests that not just marginalized but even seemingly powerful groups can be characterized by a lack of reflexivity. Quoting Mitchell and Green's (2002) study of young working-class British mothers, he argues that while they had access to some forms of reflexivity such as plastic sexuality and emphasis on individualism, they were still limited by structural constraints. His arguments imply that when the social environment endorses reflexivity and individualism, individuals attempt to practise it, but this practice does not necessarily undermine the structural conditions which impinge on them. Thus 'reflexivity does not necessarily bring choice, just a painful awareness of the lack of it' (Adams, 2006: 525). Finally Adams (2006: 519) argues that reflexivity can act as a form of regulation and as a tool to disempower individuals, as in the work context where it becomes a 'management tool for self-regulation and surveillance'. Reflexivity can be used to disadvantage some at the expense of others and to reinforce these relative advantages and disadvantages. It can be used for masking structural inequalities in the labour market and in society. In this analysis, Adams tends to focus on the darker sides of reflexivity, in a bid to refute Giddens' optimism about its emancipatory potential.

Adams alerts us to the idea that 'the construction of the self as an empowered, liberated agent is itself the unreflexive product of a particular cultural tradition; namely Western modernity.' He reminds us of the darker side of reflexivity, which has been overlooked by the reflexive modernity thesis. The popularity of notions of reflexivity can position individual decisions that are taken in the face of structural constraints as choices, thus masking inequalities based on class, race and gender. Adam's arguments indicate that reflexivity is not uniformly emancipatory and that some forms of reflexivity may even hinder the cause of individual freedom. In the empirical chapters of this book, I will examine how the valourization of individual choice can itself serve to mask the manner in which choices are constrained and limited.

Mead: The social nature of reflexivity

There are two key implications of the two alternatives to Giddens discussed above: firstly, that reflexivity is not uniformly emancipatory and empowering as Giddens' celebratory stance implies, and secondly, that the social continues to play a major role in determining the limits and opportunities of reflexivity. Taking up the significance of the social, we now turn to Mead's theories which enable a return to the social in discussing reflexivity. Recently, both Adams (2003) and Jackson (2008) have argued for the value of using Mead's notion of the self in understanding how individuals engage with the social. As Jackson argues, his work is particularly useful to feminist examinations of reflexivity as it 'offers valuable insights into the construction of gendered and sexual selves' (Jackson, 2010: 124).

According to Mead the self 'is essentially a social structure, and it arises in social experience'; that is, it is constituted when individuals begin to see themselves as an object through the eyes of others; this objective attitude or the 'self-consciousness' (as opposed to consciousness which is simply an experience) then leads to socially appropriate conduct (1934: 140). Mead's self is thus socially grounded through shared attitudes. Shared attitudes of the 'generalized other' are communicated through language, a system of symbols with commonly understood meanings (1934: 154). As a full-fledged or 'organic' member of society, the individual reflects the attitudes and institutions of the social group; the mind of the individual and the very act of thinking are socially constituted. From Mead's point of view it is impossible for individuals to reflexively construct themselves except by engaging the norms, values and ideas that are available to them within their culture.

Mead (1934) argues that individuals are engaged in continuous reflection on themselves as objects in the eyes of others while engaged in social interactions. This implies a reflexive understanding of self in the previous moment which the individual subject produces in the present moment: the creation of a coherent narrative of identity that Giddens discusses. The creation of an individual's self-identity is an ongoing reflexive process of looking at the past and the future from the standpoint of the present (Jackson, 2008). The 'me' of an individual represents the internalized set of shared attitudes which enables individuals to engage in an internal conversation about their appearance in the eyes of others. This is a form of reflexivity, but unlike Gidden's reflexivity which implies emancipation from social structure, Mead's reflexivity is deeply engaged with the social.

Mead recognizes the potential of individuals to resist social control and create change. Although he does not use the term 'agency', Mead recognizes the capacity of individuals to bring about social change and their need to be themselves, that is, to express socially inappropriate attitudes and behaviours in certain contexts. He suggests that with greater levels of complexity in society, the scope of individuality increases; however, the maintenance of complex social relations depends on the existence of autonomous individual selves.

If we agree that Giddens does indeed overplay the potential of reflexivity for enhancing individual agency and undermines the significance of social resources in shaping the self, then Mead's pragmatist theory offers an alternative socially grounded reflexivity. By adopting Mead's ideas we need not sacrifice the emancipatory potential of reflexivity. While Mead himself does not address power, gender and other structural factors, his theory of the self does not close off possibilities of understanding the structural constraints that impinge on an individual's reflexivity. It also allows for an analysis of how individuals strategize in order to overcome structural constraints and, as Chapter 7 will argue, how individual choice and responsibility can become a discourse that individuals draw on to create a reflexive narrative of self-identity. When we consider modernity in Asia, and its consequences for women, the notion of a socially constituted reflexivity is especially valuable.

Conclusion

I conclude this examination of the reflexivity thesis and its critiques by suggesting a fusion of feminist and Southern perspectives. Such a critique would not only be powerful in itself, simultaneously interrogating the Eurocentric and masculinist biases of the reflexivity thesis, but would also be relevant to the practice of sociology in an interconnected and globalized world. As the discipline of sociology matures in the 21st century, the need to provincialize European sociology and question its false universalisms becomes imperative (Connell, 2008). Therefore an empirical examination of women's experiences in the context of globalization in India should not hesitate to critique theories that proceed from European contexts.

Modernity in Asia is strongly influenced by colonial experiences as a result of which nations tend to construct their identities with reference to European modernity(ies). A colonial or postcolonial nation tends to both adopt and reject aspects of European modernity in creating its identity. Nations might aspire to technological progress, development and rational scientific temper whilst rejecting the individualism and materialism that are widely believed to be represented by European modernity. In their pursuit of modernity, nations tend to develop a heightened consciousness of tradition and attempt to preserve, revive or even create traditions that distinguish their modernity from European forms of modernity.

Modernity itself may contain conditions which have contradictory consequences for women. As Jackson (2008) argues, it would be shortsighted to conclude that Asian women's participation in paid labour, rising age of marriage or falling fertility rates indicate that they are hurtling towards a form of individualization that Giddens describes. Instead it is important to examine how they engage with the discourses of late modernity, including individualization, egalitarianism in intimate relationships and individual choice, within the framework of traditional gendered expectations associated with their positions as women in post-colonial globalizing cultures. In the following chapters, I investigate how the value of individualism is understood by Indian women and how they engage with it in creating their self-identities.

When we account for women's unique relationship with modernity in a postcolonial context, we can further strengthen and extend the feminist critique of modernity. We can see that the consequences of modernity are not merely gendered but that gender and geography can create unique consequences for women's relationship with modernity. In Chapter 3, I examine this relationship between women and modernity in India from the colonial period to the current period of globalization. I specifically concentrate on middle class women, the constituency of my research and the ostensible beneficiaries of globalization. I suggest that modernity in India is gendered in culturally specific ways that are deeply influenced by the colonial experience and also by the need to preserve a national identity in the globalized world.

3
The 'New' Indian Middle Class Woman

As I argued in the introduction, Indian sociologists have, until recently, been wary of examining the middle classes. Sociology as a discipline has historically been identified with the concerns of the less privileged members of society, making its practitioners reluctant to turn the spotlight on a class that until recently consisted largely of the upper castes. It might also be possible that Indian sociologists have tended to overlook the sociological relevance of the class to which many of them belonged. Recently, however, sociologists have begun to recognize the influential role that the middle classes play in India, particularly in creating and strengthening dominant discourses of gender, nationhood and modernity (Deshpande, 2003; Mankekar, 1999; Fernandes, 2006; Thapan, 2004). In addition the middle classes' emergence as a class of consumers is becoming increasingly evident as is the emergence of discourses around the idea of the new Indian (middle class) woman.

The class that is popularly known as the Indian middle class is believed to have emerged from the British efforts to create a class of administrators, clerical workers and translators in India who would act as interpreters and intermediaries between the colonial administration and the masses (Varma, 1998; Misra, 1961 in Jafferlot and Van der Veer, 2008). The birth of the middle class is often traced from Macaulay's famous Minute on Indian Education, which suggested that the consolidation of British power in India required the Empire 'to raise up an English-educated middle class who may be interpreters between us and the millions whom we govern – a class of persons Indian in colour, in blood but English in tastes, in opinions, in morals and in intellect' (Jafferlot and Van der Veer, 2008: 14; Varma, 1998).

The historical emergence of the middle classes via colonial rule is important to understand its relationship with modernity, but it is not to be supposed that a middle class did not exist in pre-colonial India. Earlier discussions on the middle class identified it as the class that benefited from the British need for interpreters, who received an English-language education, exposure to European ideals and professional qualifications such as law, medicine and teaching (Misra, 1961 in Jafferlot and Van der Veer, 2008; Varma, 1998). These writers saw the middle class as a class that had distanced itself from the Indian masses through language, education and lifestyle and was caught in the futile exercise of trying to mimic the colonial masters.

Ironically for the British, a large section of this class went on to lead the movement for independence, deriving at least a part of their philosophy from Enlightenment ideals such as liberty, equality and democracy. As Ray and Baviskar (2011: 5–6) point out, 'to be middle class [in this period] was to inhabit a particular orientation of modernity. It meant being open-minded and egalitarian; following the rule of law and not being swayed by private motive or particularistic agenda; being fiscally prudent and living within one's means; and embracing science and rationality in the public sphere.' The national movement was not an exclusively middle class movement, but its vision and direction came from English-speaking middle class professionals. The middle classes of the colonial period emerged not only from the intelligentsia but also from small business owners, traders and merchants (Jafferlot and Van der Veer, 2008). In caste terms the middle classes comprised Brahamins and Banias, that is, priests and traders (both upper castes). This is now changing as more and more depressed castes join the middle classes based on their increasing economic and political power. Thus the middle classes are more than just the intelligentsia, and their contribution to nation building has gone much further than merely imitating the West or administering India on behalf of the colonial masters (Fernandes, 2006; Jafferlot and Van der Veer, 2008).

By providing the vision and leadership for the national movement, the middle classes acquired a certain moral legitimacy to envisage and direct the progress of the nation (Deshpande, 2003). In the earlier years following independence, they did so by participating in political life and administration and through their continued dominance of professional occupations. In this period the middle class upheld the notion of a developmental state. National progress was identified with a socialist state, command economy and centralized planning. The state supported the growth of large industries and technological progress whilst the middle classes provided the scientific, technical knowledge and administrative skill required for the nation's development. The nationalist vision for self-reliance resulted in the promotion of Indian industry and continued boycott of foreign goods (Deshpande, 2003; Varma, 1998).

In the late 20th and early 21st centuries, however, the middle classes have begun to identify with the discourse of globalization, supporting the notion that India can become a dominant player in the world market through a capitalist free-market economy (Deshpande, 2003; Fernandes, 2006; Varma, 1998). Since the economic liberalization process began in 1991, middle class entrepreneurs, business professionals and government servants have collaborated with the government to position India both nationally and internationally as an emerging economy with high potential for growth thanks to a large pool of English-speaking, technically qualified labour; low production costs; a relatively stable, reform-oriented government; and rising consumer aspirations (see, for instance, the website of the Indian Brand Equity Foundation: http://www.ibef.org). The emergence of India as an important player in the world economy and its success in attracting foreign investment have increased the middle classes' confidence and boosted its self-image as representatives of the nation (Varma, 1998; Deshpande, 2003).

Today consumption plays an important role in India as it is associated with the nation's prosperity and progress. If large dams were symbolic of a newly independent, developing nation in the 1950s and 1960s, then today's symbols of national development could be cell phones, laptops and indigenous as well as international brands of cars. As the middle classes engage in their consumerist aspirations within the borders of the nation, 'commodities weave together narratives of nationhood and development with the creation of middle class identity' (Fernandes, 2006: 41).

The optimism around globalization and the desire to attract foreign investment in the 1990s led to an overestimation of the spending capacity of the middle classes. Although the penetration of electronic goods, cars and motorcycles and household appliances has increased across urban India, it is still much less than that of established economies and repeat purchases are rare. Nevertheless easy access to credit, hire-purchase schemes and the availability of global brands have increased the middle class's appetite for consumption. It is eager to spend the unprecedented incomes that it earns through privatization and participation in the transnational economy. Even if actual levels of consumption are much lower than estimated, consumption has become a defining feature of middle class identities (Fernandes, 2006; Jafferlot and Van der Veer, 2008), extending from goods, services, entertainment and leisure pursuits to education, health care and political ideologies.

In this chapter I examine the discursive production of the notion of the 'new Indian middle class woman' which is closely related to middle class discourses on globalization and modernity. The manner in which this discourse is produced cannot be understood outside of the middle classes' relationship with modernity, a modernity which, as I suggested in Chapter 2, is both culturally specific and highly gendered. The discourses around middle class women were created in the colonial period and through the nationalist movement. They were influenced by the autonomous women's movement of the 1970s and 1980s, the neoliberal policies of 1990s and the rise of hegemonic Hinduism in the same period. They need to be examined in this historical context. Before doing so, however, it is important to explore some indicators by which middle class identities may be defined in contemporary India.

Defining the Indian middle classes

Two of the greatest challenges in estimating the size of the middle class are the optimism around globalization and its desirability as a social identity which cause its size to be exaggerated. Given the association of middle class identities with the values of hard work, moral probity and moderation, individuals from across the social hierarchy tend to claim a middle class identity. While it remains a desirable social identity (Deshpande, 2003), some of the optimism of globalization has been moderated in the light of economic recession. Recent estimates from the NCAER indicate that it consists of 31.4 million households or 160 million people and forms about 13% of India's population. It is predicted that this number will grow to about 53.3 million households or 267 million people by 2015 (NCAER in *The Economic Times*, 2011). However, since fieldwork for this book took place in 2006 and 2007, NCAER's estimates from 2005 are more pertinent in defining the Indian middle classes. The NCAER's 2005 typology of consumer classes, adapted in Table 3.1, takes into account the internal diversity in the middle classes by dividing them into upper, lower and middle factions. The descriptors of the categories in the original classification were in Sanskrit. In this typology they have been loosely translated into English to facilitate easier understanding.

Economic indicators

From Table 3.1 it is evident that the middle classes fall into the income bracket of Rs 200,000 to about Rs 2,000,000. Although it might be argued

Table 3.1   Income categories in India

Categories[a]	Descriptors	Annual income in Rupees	Annual income in US dollars at an approximate exchange rate of Rs 50 to 1 USD (2005 values)	No. of households in 2005–2006
A	Very rich	Greater than 10,000,001	Greater than 200,000	52,000
B	Rich	5,000,001–10,000,000	100,000–200,000	103,000
C	Nearly rich	2,000,001–5,000,000	40,000–100,000	454,000
D	Upper middle class	1,000,001–2,000,000	20,000–40,000	1,122,000
E	Middle class	500,001–1,000,000	10,000–20,000	3,212,000
F	Lower middle class	200,001–500,000	4,000–10,000	13,183,000
G	Working class	91,000–200,000	1,820–4,000	53,276,000
H	Poor	Less than 90,000	Less than 1,820	132,249,000

[a] Descriptors of the categories in the original classification were in Sanskrit. In this typology they have been loosely translated into English to facilitate easier understanding.
Source: Adapted from the NCAER classification 2005.[1]

that households with an income of Rs 2,000,000 are closer to the rich than the middle classes, I would suggest that households in that income bracket are likely to share the middle class values and identities of those whose incomes are a few hundred thousand rupees lower. When the income of the Indian middle classes is converted from rupees to US dollars, however, it becomes evident that an income which in the USA would barely obtain basic necessities is enough to create a middle class lifestyle in India.

Economic definitions of the Indian middle class that are based on household income are useful in estimating the size of the middle class but do not account for the manner in which households move across the class hierarchy over a period of time and fail to explain the exchange of goods and money between households, especially those related through blood and marriage. For instance, young professionals, married couples and students may receive help from their parents and other family members in setting up a household while elderly people may receive support from their grown-up children. Families may move from the lower to the upper middle class on the strength of one member's income or may fall from the upper to the lower middle class when the main wage earner retires. Finally, when considering class in India, we need to account for the flexible nature of Indian households, the close financial ties between family members living in separate households and moral obligations between parents and children (see Chapters 4 and 5).

When calculating household income, expenditure is usually taken as a proxy for income. However, this method is not without flaws. When individuals move up and down the hierarchy of income categories, they might continue to follow the lifestyle of the social class that they have just left. One participant in my research, Meenakshi, is a case in point. Living alone in a one-person household at the time when we met, she had an annual income Rs. 140,000, which suggests that she is from the working class. However, her description of her parents' home in Kerala (her father was a retired government employee) indicates that the latter may be classified as middle class. She was going through a divorce during my fieldwork, but when she was married, her joint income with her (former) husband would have put her in the upper middle class category. Since her parents support her when required, she is in a position to continue engaging in some of the leisure pursuits and activities that she followed while married and to socialize (occasionally) with friends whose incomes are much higher than hers. Thus her expenditure suggests an upper middle class lifestyle. The ambiguities of her class position indicate that while economic classifications are useful as background data to give a broader picture of the conditions within which individuals live, they are not in themselves adequate to define the middle class.

Socio-cultural indicators

Given the limitations of income as an indicator in defining the middle classes, we need to look at other (non-economic) forms of capital that define the middle classes. Middle class privilege is often founded on the ability to accumulate and deploy several forms of cultural capital, including education, fluency in English and access to technical and professional qualifications as well as more intangible attributes such as a cosmopolitan outlook, the ability to interact with people outside of one's caste group, exposure to metropolitan lifestyles and familiarity with a broader range of cultures and languages. Andre Bétteille (1993: 44) argues that the transfer of cultural capital is 'guided by complex social and psychological processes whose outcome is never guaranteed', but the emotional, financial and social investments that middle class parents make in their children have definite consequences for their success. It is usually the upper middle classes who are in a better position to access and transfer these investments, which may range from supervising their children's schooling, sending them to coaching classes, encouraging their talents in sport or in the arts, providing them with books and other educational resources and motivating them to achieve.

Recent research such as the ethnography of the IT industry under-taken by Upadhya and Vasavi (2006) and Krishna and Brihmadesam's (2006) investigation of the socio-economic backgrounds of IT workers has found that, since these attributes are particularly valuable in the tran-snational job market, those who have an urban, metropolitan upbring-ing, university-educated parents and exposure outside of their home state are more likely to benefit from the opportunities created by economic liberalization than others. Leela Fernandes (2006) in her broader inves-tigation of the impact of economic liberalization on the middle classes found that there is a definite distinction between those who inherit the cultural capital necessary for success in the global economy and those who are struggling to acquire it through a variety of targeted educa-tional programmes ranging from 'personality development classes' to MBA degrees.

To understand the importance of cultural capital in strengthening mid-dle class status, it is useful to think in terms of two generations. Families belonging to the middle and upper middle class are in a better position to transmit cultural capital to their children than the lower middle class and working class. Economic liberalization in the 1990s increased pri-vatization and the growth of industry has resulted in upward mobility across the middle classes. Those who grew up in the middle to upper ranks of the middle classes have the requisite cultural capital to take on top managerial positions, thereby not only consolidating their middle class status but also moving closer to the elite. However, individuals who grew up in the lower to the middle ranks of the middle class, or even in working-class backgrounds, have also found employment in the pri-vate sector albeit in non-management-track positions. Having acquired much less cultural capital growing up, they tend to take on short-term contractual positions which are less secure and have limited possibili-ties for growth (Fernandes, 2006). Given the insecurities inherent in the free-market economy, and the threat of recession, the middle classes are constantly faced with the possibility of retrenchment. Consequently their status as upper, middle or lower middle class is to some extent inse-cure, although this insecurity is probably most keenly felt in the middle to lower ranks of the middle classes who also lack the necessary cultural capital to strengthen their relatively new middle class status.

To further elucidate the relationship between middle class status and cultural capital, it is useful to adapt Gurcharan Das's distinction between the old and new middle class to our purpose. Das (2000: 290) describes the new middle class as having recently migrated from rural to urban areas (possibly one generation ago). He describes the new middle class as conspicuous in its consumption and professionally ambitious, having 'less hypocrisy and more self-confidence', while the old middle class, he argues, consists of individuals whose parents worked in the public sector or well-established private companies, grew up in urban metropolitan India and studied in well-established English-medium schools. Rejecting the polemical aspects of this definition, we may still retain the distinction of new and old middle classes by drawing from the empirical research of Fernandes (2006), Krishna and Brihmadesam (2006) and Upadhya and Vasavi (2006). Old middle classes may be described as those who have inherited the cultural capital necessary for success in the globalized economy from their families while new middle classes would be those who are attempting to gain the same cultural capital by deploying economic capital. The middle class status of the former might be considered to be more entrenched while that of the latter, being of relatively recent origin, is more precarious.

The terms 'new middle class' and 'old middle class' suggest that there is some fluidity in an individual's or family's middle class status over generations. They also enable a shift from definitions of middle class based solely on income to those based on cultural capital; that is, hypothetically a family that might be middle or upper middle class in terms of income is new middle class in terms of cultural capital and lifestyle. However, by and large, the old middle class will be largely concentrated in the upper ranks of the middle class while the new middle class will be largely concentrated in the lower to middle ranks of the middle class in terms of income. This distinction may be usefully applied in Chapter 5 which discusses the emotional and social investments that middle class families make in the success of their daughters and daughters-in-law.

The middle classes' relationship with modernity

The Indian middle classes are often criticized for their 'mistaken modernity' (Gupta, 2000), their focus on their own self-interest (Varma, 1998) and their fascination with Europe and the West which has caused them to culturally distance themselves from the nation. It has been suggested that while they are obsessed with the technological artefacts and lifestyle that connotes 'modernity', they ignore its ideals: rationality, democracy, equality, value accorded to achievement over birth and broader human concerns over the parochialisms of family, community and caste. Gupta (2000) argues that the middle classes strengthen their own position of privilege by embracing traditional norms and practices such as casteism, paternalism and religiosity that might be exploitative of their less privileged compatriots. While many of Gupta's criticisms of the middle class may be justified, his definition of modernity in terms of 'dignity of the individual', 'adherence to universalistic norms', 'elevation of individual achievement over privileges or disprivileges of birth' and 'accountability in public life' overlooks many inegalitarian practices that occur in so-called 'modern (Western) societies' as well as the colonial experience through which India first encountered (European) modernity.

In Chapter 2 I argued via Bhambra and Connell that European modernity cannot be understood without reference to the (physical, psychological and cultural) oppression of colonialism. In this chapter I draw on Yoko Hayami, Akio Tanabe and Yumiko Tokita-Tanabe's (2003) argument that modernity in postcolonial nations needs to be understood in relation to the colonial experience. They argue that the development of the (European) colonizer's self-construction as the epitome of modernity and rationality required the construction of the colonized as exotic, traditional, chaotic and corporeal. However, this construction was internalized by the colonized people so that their own self-concept was influenced by it. In colonized nations modernity became associated with power and autonomy on the one hand and with oppression on the other. It therefore became both a goal to strive for and a value to define one's self against. Modernity in postcolonial nations needs to be understood in terms of this mutual tendency to create an 'Other' on the part of both the colonizer and the colonized. To understand modernity in colonial and postcolonial contexts, we need to take into account a number of 'dichotomous frameworks such as modern: traditional, West: East, colonizer: colonized, rational: emotional, mind: body and public: domestic' that are associated with it (Hayami, Tanabe and Tokita-Tanabe, 2003) where the West is constructed as rational, cognitive and masculine while the East is emotive, corporeal and feminine. This cultural essentialization obliterates similarities between the colonizers and the colonized as well as diversities within each. The colonized culture has a special stake in this cultural essentialism. It tends to respond to the humiliation of colonialism by selectively valorizing its own traditions while engaging in a project of modernization (Jayawardena, 2002; Chatterjee, 1989; Pollard, 2005).[2] The manner in which history, tradition, gender and national identity are constructed in colonial and postcolonial cultures needs to be understood in this context.

Given these characteristics of colonial and postcolonial modernities, how might we understand the Indian middle classes' relationship with modernity? Like any colonized people they viewed themselves and their culture through the colonial gaze, internalizing both the criticisms of the colonizers and their fascination with India's cultural heritage. These two seemingly opposite tendencies are evident in the movements for reform and revival that accompanied the nationalist movement in the late 19th and early 20th centuries. The reformists turned a critical lens on traditional practices such as caste, child marriage and sati (immolation of widows), seeking to remodel Hinduism on the lines of Christianity and other monotheistic religions, denouncing idol worship, superstitions and the dominance of priestly castes. The revivalists sought a pristine national culture within ancient Vedic traditions, leading to a selective reinterpretation of Hindu scriptures and mythology. On the one hand Vedic texts were revived in an attempt to trace the past of the nation and give it a defined identity while, on the other, middle class nationalists aspired to the Enlightenment ideals of liberty, democracy and equality. These trends were not always as contradictory as they seemed, as their goal was to create a sovereign nation based on a common identity. Their vision for an independent India was for it to engage on an equal footing with the more powerful nations of the West whilst also embodying a uniquely Indian modernity that was distinctive in terms of certain cultural traditions. In this manner they laid the foundation for the Indian middle classes' relationship with modernity and tradition through the 20th and 21st centuries.

Given this legacy in their relationship with modernity, the contemporary Indian middle class is not mistakenly modern, nor do they evoke tradition only from the point of view of self-interest. Rather the middle class is keen to distinguish its modernity from the dominant models of modernity embodied by Europe and the northern hemisphere (with which it inevitably shares some common characteristics). While their relatively successful engagement in the global market has raised the Indian middle classes' self-confidence and dimmed the memories of colonialism, they continue to define their modernity by selectively invoking certain traditional ideals, norms and practices as intrinsically good and worth preserving. As Deshpande (2003) remarks, the phrase 'perfect blend of tradition and modernity' has become something of a cliché in India. Whether real or imagined, invented or resurrected, tradition is used to define the cultural specificity of Indian modernity and distance it from the modernity of the West. Recalling Thompson (1996) from the previous chapter it may be argued that this identity-affirming aspect of tradition makes it a vital component of the uniquely Indian modernity that the middle classes aspire to create. However, this uniquely Indian modernity cannot be easily defined or pinned down since it is highly contextual. Depending on the context, middle class Indians construct their modernity by repeatedly 'othering' the West or even their own compatriots as too cosmopolitan, too parochial, too Westernized, too Indian, too conservative or too liberated (Favero, 2005).

The 'women's question' in colonial and postcolonial India

The nationalist debates on Indian womanhood

Within the debates on modernity and national identity in colonial and postcolonial nations, women become 'the symbolic bearers of the collectivity's identity and honour', and their position becomes indicative of the nation's modernity (Yuval-Davis, 1997: 45). The position of women becomes a contentious issue between the colonizer and the colonized and between reformers and revivalists within the colonized nation. In nationalist thought, women become 'symbolic "border guards"' who not only transmit and uphold cultural values but also need to be protected as the violation of their honour challenges the (manhood of the) nation (Armstrong, 1982 in Yuval-Davis, 1997: 23). Debates around the question of veiling and unveiling in Egypt occurred within this context (Pollard, 2005; Ahmed, 1992). In Uganda nationalist discourses were fused with the question of protecting women's sexuality against exploitation by British colonizers and Indian traders (Obbo, 1989). In Indonesia colonial rule and missionary activity reduced women's economic and sexual autonomy, reforming their position through a European education that underlined domesticity (Ramusack and Sievers, 1999) while retaining certain Javanese values. Although women sometimes participate in the construction of their identity as cultural reproducers to gain authority and prestige (Yuval-Davis, 1997), their voices, whether of assent or dissent, are usually muted by more powerful forces.

In India, for instance, questions of sati (widow burning), child marriage and enforced widowhood were debated between the colonial administration and the Indians they governed, and amongst the Indian nationalists themselves. However, the voices of women on these issues, and those of depressed castes, were frequently drowned out in the 19th and 20th centuries (with some noteworthy exceptions discussed later). Both Lata Mani (1989) and Gayatri Spivak (1985/1999), despite the differences in their approach, have shown that the subjectivities and experiences of the women who were the targets of these customs rarely figure in the debate, although the customs themselves are used to indict the culture of the colony – see Spivak's (1999: 284) famous statement on 'white men saving brown women from brown men'. The debate seems to have been largely middle class (unsurprising since the customs of sati and child marriage were largely middle class/upper caste) but occurred as if it was relevant to all Indian women, the participants rarely recognizing their class/caste bias. While it is important to recognize the tremendous challenges faced by working-class women in pre-independent and independent India, for the purpose of this book, I examine the impact of this middle class-centric debate on the discursive construction of Indian womanhood.

Amongst revivalists the construction of ideal Indian womanhood was part of the attempt to essentialize Indian culture and conflate it with Hinduism. They repeatedly evoked the idea of a golden age of Vedic Hinduism wherein women were revered and accorded a high status (Chakravarti, 1989). Scriptural evidence of women's equality with men was amassed, and lesser known mythical figures such as Maitreyee and Gargi believed to personify female intellectual achievement were revived (Chakravarti, 1989). Sita, Savitri, Sati and Yashoda, mythical archetypes of wifely devotion and selfless motherhood, were upheld for women to emulate.

While the reformists opposed practices that were discriminatory towards women, such as child marriage, seclusion of widows, sati and purdah (seclusion of women), they were careful not to directly challenge the Hindu elite. Women's education was planned with a view to develop housekeeping skills, inculcate scientific attitudes and reinforce their roles as transmitters of pristine Indian culture (Chatterjee, 1989). They were encouraged to pursue 'the goal of cultural refinement' through a new body of vernacular literature developed for this purpose (Chatterjee, 1989: 246). This attempt at inculcating scientific temper and modernization in women's education while preventing unchecked Westernization continued to characterize attitudes towards women's education in independent India.

In his popular work on the subject, Partha Chatterjee argues that the 19th-century home was recast as a pure, idyllic space where educated Indian men could retire from serving or fighting their colonial masters to wives who supported their Westernized lifestyle while upholding Indian traditions. Women were to be educated to act as intellectual companions to men whilst also maintaining the sanctity of the home by performing religious rituals, following traditions and passing cultural knowledge to their children (Chatterjee, 1989). They were encouraged to adopt markers of modernity in domestic roles – 'orderliness, thrift, cleanliness and a personal sense of responsibility, the practical skills of accounting, hygiene and the ability to run the household according to the new physical and economic conditions set by the outside world' (Chatterjee, 1989: 247). Chatterjee argues that the nationalists resolved the question of a woman's participation in public life by suggesting that she may do so if her traditionalism and Indianness were indicated through culturally visible '"spiritual" qualities in her dress, her eating habits, her social demeanour and her religiosity' (Chatterjee, 1989: 247–248).

Chatterjee has been criticized for generalizing the experience of a small regional and caste group (Bengali Brahamins) to women across India and for ignoring both male and female social reformers' criticism of Brahminism (Nair, 2011; Rege, 1998). Upper caste female reformers of the 19th century such as Pandita Ramabai (1888/2000) protested against the Brahmanical treatment of women, writing scathing indictments against the Hindu scriptures on which many oppressive customary laws were based. Comparing the plight of high caste women to their working-class sisters she asserted that the latter are better off as 'they are obliged to depend on themselves, an opportunity for self-reliance is afforded to them … [while high caste women remain] helpless victims of indolence and false timidity" (Ramabai/Kosambi, 1888/2000: 172). Others such as Tarabai Shinde (1882/2010) strongly criticized the culture's double standards and hypocrisy in its treatment of women. Both women suggested that not only was the freedom of upper caste women highly restricted, but they were also subjected to inhuman treatment by their male relatives. Jyotiba Phule, a key male figure in the 19th century reform movement, was also known for his sympathy for women. He saw women's education as essential both for social reform and for their own emancipation. His support of the cause is evident in his establishment of a school for girls from the depressed castes and his campaign for the rights of widows along with his wife Savtrabai Phule (Guha, 2010).

In the 20th century a range of women's magazines edited by newly literate middle class women in Bengal, Kerala and in (what is now) Uttar Pradesh, Tamil Nadu and Maharashtra debated the role of women in the emerging nation (see Awaya, 2003; Talwar, 1989). For most part, the editorial line of the journals exhorted women to avoid imitating the West and preserve their national identity through devotion to their families. The nation was projected as an extension of the family, and women's role as citizens included raising healthy children for the motherland, inculcating patriotism and spiritual values in them and supporting husbands and brothers through compliance and spirituality (Awaya, 2003; Chakravarti, 1989). However, they also questioned their subordinate status in the home and in the nationalist movement. Writing in Malayalam in *Sarada* (named after the Hindu Goddess of Learning) in the mid-1920s, C. Narayanikkutti Amma criticized the traditional maxim of blind devotion to husband, questioning the contemporary relevance of ancient role models such as Sita and Savitri (Awaya, 2003). Similar sentiments were reiterated by Uma Nehru in the Hindi magazine *Stree Darpan* (Women's Mirror) in 1918. She demanded why a nation that aspires to create Western economic and political systems expects its women to conform to indigenous traditions (Talwar, 1989).

However, the most definitive contradiction of the discourse that placed women at home came from women's active participation in the various movements for independence. While the male nationalists were at first reluctant to recruit women on the frontlines, they soon realized the importance of doing so. In the early years of his leadership Gandhi suggested that women's best contribution would be within the home (through spinning cotton and providing inspiration to men). However, based on demands from women themselves and on seeing them lead and direct the movement when the male leaders were jailed, he began to encourage their public participation (Forbes, 1996). Women carried messages, nursed the wounded and provided organizational help; they participated in public marches and were arrested in the nationalist cause (Mankekar, 1999; Liddle and Joshi, 1986). By the Civil Disobedience movement of the 1930s, nationalist leaders had begun to recognize both the symbolic and practical advantages of women's active participation in the movement. Female revolutionaries (who were outside Gandhi's non-violent movement) also played an active part in destabilizing the colonial regime (Forbes, 1996).

Ambedkar, one of Gandhi's staunchest critics, saw the oppression of women as closely related to caste oppression (Guha, 2010). He supported self-determination for women, especially in the area of marriage, seeing it as the one of the key ways to annihilate caste (Gaikwad, 2010). Soon after independence, as law minister, he drafted the Hindu code bill which sought to empower women by allowing divorce and giving women rights of inheritance in family property. These sweeping reforms to Hindu personal law, vehemently opposed at the time, have nevertheless been passed with modifications in subsequent years.

In discussing the diversity of perspectives that came from both men and women, I have attempted to suggest that 'the women's question' was not easily resolved. Though the 19th-century nationalist discourse might have attempted to restrict women's public presence, by the 20th century the leaders were unable to enforce these restrictions on women's agency in defining their own positions in an emerging nation. The tension between the male leadership's view of women's roles in the nationalist movement and the realities of their struggle indicates the potential for emancipation within the discourse. Although women's education was planned around the agenda of selective modernization, once they were educated many began to question the central tenets of their education, as the diverse views in the editorial lines of women's magazines indicate. They began to find opportunities for higher education and for participating in public life. Political life and the press became arenas for reinforcing, questioning, and at times, even subverting the discourse. However, women's engagement in the nationalist movement came at a price: they could not criticize the existing patriarchal order without inadvertently supporting the colonial state in its indictment of Indian culture (Liddle and Joshi, 1986). This constraint diluted the intensity with which women's issues were taken up. The cause of women's emancipation was kept subordinate to that of emancipating the nation.

The discourse of 'respectable modernity' and the 'new' Indian woman

The arrival of the 'new' Indian woman

The above discussion suggests that discourses of gender and nationhood tend to be closely interconnected, especially in the Indian context. The discursive construction of ideal womanhood in postcolonial India continues to be influenced by the conflation of women with tradition and spirituality, although some distinct differences from the nationalist construction of Indian womanhood are evident. As I argued in the beginning of this chapter, the Rajiv Gandhi-led Congress government began to support middle class aspirations in the mid-1980s, not only by giving impetus to consumerism but also by supporting education and technological development. Several industries were deregulated and the tax on consumer goods was reduced. The government attempted to raise revenues for the state-controlled television network Doordarshan by encouraging private sponsorship of programmes.

A national-level project for 'the uplift of women' was undertaken by the state-controlled television network with numerous programmes aired on TV being targeted at women. These included not just fictional television serials but programmes on educating women on their legal rights, on health and hygiene and on parenting. However, as Purnima Mankekar's (1999) ethnology of television narratives and their audiences in the late eighties and early nineties found, women's independence was often contained within patriarchal families and communities. When they exercised agency it was usually for the public good rather than for individual progress.

The emerging consumerism of the middle classes made an additional income essential to the family's comfort and economic stability. It may be argued that the realities of economic life destabilized the cultural notion of women as anchored within the home. However, women were going outside their homes for the sake of their families' well-being, not for their own independence; thus, their professional status did not mean that they had opted out of family life or kinship ties. Mankekar (1999) gives an example from amongst her interviewees of the eldest daughter of a lower middle class family whose income was so important to her family's survival that her marriage was delayed, causing much tension between father and daughter. This example indicates that employment could be both enabling and constraining, causing a degree of ambivalence towards women's employment. The tension between the two generations' views on education and employment, the conflict between cultural notions that situate women in the home and the economic realities that require her to enter the workplace became the foundation on which the constructions of womanhood emerged in the post-liberalization, globalization period: the 1990s and the new millennium.

Alongside these trends of consumerism, the autonomous women's movement emerged – autonomous because the cause of women's liberation was now sought independently from other issues faced by the nation. While women had been participating in various movements since independence, these reached critical mass in the late 1970s. This was fuelled in part by the publication of *Towards Equality* – a report by the Committee on the Status of Women in 1974 which stated in unequivocal terms that the constitutional guarantee of equality for women had not been achieved in independent India. In particular it highlighted the situation of working-class and rural women.

The autonomous women's movement sought legal and social sanctions against rape, dowry and domestic violence. The custom of taking dowries from brides' families at a wedding which had been confined to a few communities in pre-colonial times spread across caste and regional lines in the colonial and postcolonial period (Oldenberg, 2010). In the 1970s and 1980s growing consumerist aspirations amongst the middle classes led to exponential increase in demands for dowry by grooms' families. Demands included cars, scooters, household goods, electronic equipment, clothes, jewellery, property and money. When the demands were not met it often led to domestic violence, murder and suicides of young married women. In response women partici- pated in the anti-dowry movement. It has been argued that the custom of giving dowry is largely upper caste/middle class and that by taking up this issue in such strong terms the women's movement continues to remain elitist in its focus. This charge notwithstanding, advocacy by the autonomous women's movement resulted in the strengthening of anti-dowry laws.

The charge of elitism and Hindu majoritarianism both in the issues taken up and in the use of symbols has often come from within the women's movement itself. Flavia Agnes argues that by using symbols of female power such as the Hindu goddesses Durga and Shakti, the women's movement continues to equate India with Hinduism (1998). However three major events, the Shahbano case which raised the ques- tion of Muslim women's rights in marriage, the demolition of the Babri Masjid and women's active participation in the violence that accom- panied and followed it, and the participation of young 'forward caste' girls in the nation-wide agitation against the Mandal Commission which sought to enhance employment opportunities for depressed castes indicated that the women's movement needs to grapple with caste, religion and community alongside gender (Agnes, 1994; Agnihotri and Mazumdar, 1995; Tharu and Niranjana, 1996). These were difficult issues for a movement essentially concerned with building a 'sisterhood' of women to confront; they also strengthened regressive religious forces that were antithetical to rights of women.

The question of Muslim Personal Law (related to divorce and marriage settlements) came up in a prominent divorce settlement case, popularly called 'the Shahbano case' that reached the nation's Supreme Court in the mid-1980s (Patel, 1988). Although there was heated public debate around it, the final outcome was unfavourable to women. Taken together the issues of dowry and Muslim Personal Law underscored women's vulnerability in marriage, but it also showed the complexity of the issue of women's right when it becomes a matter of debate between religious extremists and reformists. In response to the issue the women's movement campaigned for a uniform civil code on marriage in place of religious/cus- tomary law, only to find that their cause was actively supported by the Hindu right whose agenda in that case was largely to undermine Muslims. Agnihotri and Mazumdar (1995: 1869) argue that 'the mid-1980s have seen an onslaught on even existing rights of women through a harking back to tradition and culture and the posting of images of women's reproductive role as the only natural historical one.'

In 1990 the women's movement was once again confronted by the prominence of young middle class women in the anti-Mandal Commission agitation which opposed caste-based reservations in government jobs. Young upper caste/middle class women took to the streets agitating not only against the perceived loss of opportunities for themselves but also for their future 'husbands', thus underlining the continued possibility of caste endogamy. A few years later the active participation of women in the demolition of the Babri Mosque and the anti-Muslim violence that followed indicated that women's public participation could take a highly communalist turn. Women leaders of right-wing religious parties set an example for participation in public life while espousing highly patriarchal views and underlining the role of women in preserving and defending traditional values.

These events and trends are important in understanding the historical circumstances under which the women I interviewed were growing up. Middle class families were beginning to realize that arranged marriages were not without risk for their daughters. Consequently they began to seriously envisage a career for their daughters and educate them with a view that they might have something to fall back on if the marriage broke down. Once they received an education, it is possible that daughters began to view their careers as a bigger priority and not just a 'fallback option'. However, these personal aspirations of the young women need to be understood within a culture where neoliberal policies fuelled the consumerist aspirations of the middle classes on the one hand and regressive religious forces were undermining the rights of women on the other.

'Respectable modernity enshrined in tradition'

In the period following economic reforms the middle classes began to take pride in the nation's integration into the global market, as suggested by the availability of global brand in consumer goods and increased job opportunities in the private sector. Even though there was a discrepancy between the middle class's spending capacity and its discursive constitution as a consuming class, consumption became a marker not only of the nation's prosperity and progress but also of middle class status. Alongside discourses of a new resurgent nation that could rival the developed nations of Europe and North America emerged the discourse of the new Indian woman.

The emergence of the new Indian middle class woman as a discursive construct is found in the print media, television, advertising and recurrent debates on morality and globalization through the 1990s. Women's magazines such as *Femina* and *Women's Era* might target old, middle class, urban, English-speaking women, but they address their readers as if they are representative of all Indian women across the lines of caste, religion, language or class. Analysing this discourse through the deconstruction of commercial advertising and television in the 1990s, Rajeshwari Sunder Rajan points to the construction of a 'new' Indian woman who is seen as 'intrinsically "modern" and "liberated"' (1993: 131). She is no longer located only in the domestic world but is active in the professional and public domains. The international women's magazine *Cosmopolitan* was launched in India in the 1990s with the strapline 'Honest, Sexy, Smart: Are You Up to It'. The price of the magazine and editorial line indicated that it was targeted at upper middle class/economically independent women, but it had an impact on the content of established English-language women's magazines in India, which addressed wider audiences; *Femina, Women's Era and Savvy* re-launched themselves to compete with the foreign glossy. In addition to fashion and glamour, the women's magazines now devote space to professional and financial concerns, intimacy, lifestyle and travel.

The post-liberalization discourse on Indian women co-opts many of feminist ideals, choice, autonomy and freedom, to recreate women as consumers and encourage their participation as workers in the transnational capitalist economy. The emancipatory potential of feminist ideas is eroded as they become part of the neoliberal vocabulary and an instrument of governmentality, but individuals do find ways to subvert even this appropriation of feminism and make space for individual autonomy as the next few chapters will argue. The emphasis on individualism, however, has another consequence, that of weakening the collective identities of 'woman' and 'worker' and eroding the possibility of collective action. As Chapters 5 and 6 indicate, old middle class women are rarely sensitive to the concerns of those who are struggling to anchor themselves in the middle class.

While the so-called 'newness of the Indian woman' is repeatedly emphasized, in many respects the post-liberalization construction of Indian womanhood is a continuation of the nationalist representation of the middle class Indian woman. Education continues to be valued for the scientific temper and broader outlook that it gives women. It is believed to facilitate her role as a companion and helpmate to her husband but must not lead to the breakdown of the family which could happen if a woman is educated 'too much' (Mankekar, 1999, quoting her interviewees). However, professional employment is additionally incorporated into the construction of the new Indian woman as an important marker of her modernity (Belliappa, 2006; Sunder Rajan, 1993).

In my analysis of female characters in Bollywood films (Belliappa, 2006), I argue that they personify confidence, self-reliance, strong commitment to career and are able to negotiate public spaces: qualities that the audience is invited to admire through the eyes of the male lead. While they are represented as individualistic in their professional ambitions and choice of mates, their individualism does not exclude a strong sense of tradition. The discourse of the new Indian woman suggests that individual self-actualization and professional success are bound with commitment to family, community or nation. Her individualism 'functions for the social good' (Sunder Rajan, 1993: 135). As Meenakshi Thapan suggests in her analysis of *Femina's* editorial message (2004: 415–416), this construction of the new Indian woman 'simultaneously portrays her as glamorous, independent, conscious of her embodiment and the many forms of adornment and self-presentation available to her, and yet enshrined in the world of tradition through her adherence to family and national values'. She represents 'respectable modernity enshrined in tradition' (Thapan, 2004: 415).

In the media women's individualism is closely bound with their ability to consume, choosing the right products and brands for themselves and their families. Women's emancipation is seen not as an outcome of political struggle but through the choices and opportunities provided to her by 'benevolent capitalist socio-economic forces' (Sunder Rajan, 1993 in Oza, 2006: 40). As a rational, confident, choice-making consumer, who is conscious of her beauty and self-presentation, the new Indian woman comes to represent the resurgence of the nation and integration into the global economy. Alongside commercials on television, print advertisements and billboards, women's magazines such as *Femina* address women as consumers, suggesting beauty, personal care and household products that they could consume, holidays that they could take and investments that they might wish to make. In spite of pan-Indian implications of the term 'new Indian woman', the very manner in which she is represented indicates that the label refers to middle or upper middle class urban women. The brands and products that are offered to her and the manner in which she is represented in films and on television and the fashion trends, garments and accessories that are offered to her indicate her economically superior status. However, in her economic and social empowerment she represents the aspirations of her less privileged compatriots. In spite of associations of glamour and beauty with the new Indian woman, there continues to be a certain tension and anxiety in the discourse regarding her sexuality. As the nation opens itself to the influence of the global economy, women's bodies and sexualities are positioned as particularly vulnerable to the permissive cultural influences of the West. Rupal Oza (2006) argues that the relative loss of national sovereignty in the face of global capitalism is projected on to women's sexualities which are more stringently controlled and regulated. The anxiety around women's purity was evident in the 1990s in opposition to the Miss Universe contest being held in India, in public debates on women's clothing, and more recently, in the violence against women in pubs by right-wing political groups. To an extent this tension is resolved by linking tradition and modernity as in the cliché 'perfect blend of tradition and modernity', but since both these categories are shifting and contextual they can often be in conflict with each other.

The discourse of the 'respectable modernity' might be tied to the emergence of the so-called 'new Indian woman' but has several elements of the earlier nationalist discourse on Indian womanhood. The new Indian woman represents the nation's modernity, its economic strength and its distinctive traditions. She is believed to embody 'Indianness' in the face of globalization. While she is less 'protected' from the West than women of the nationalist period, the new Indian woman continues to carry visible markers of 'Indianness' while she participates in the global economy and culture. She is expected to continue her commitment to home and to family relationships, especially to children. In the empirical chapters of this book I examine how some of these expectations influence women's lived realities. In Chapter 7 I shall revisit the discourse of respectable modernity to investigate how it influences women's construction of self.

Conclusion

The question arises, how do individual middle class women make sense of such discourses in their daily lives? Recent research on contemporary middle class women indicates that their identities derive from both their confidence in public spaces such as the workplace and their commitment to family. Tokita-Tanabe's research in Bhubaneshwar, a small town of eastern India, suggests that the collective gaze of family and community influences the construction of their self-identities: these women create their unique identity by otherizing rural women (perceived as too shy and traditional) and metropolitan women (dismissed as too Westernized), claiming that only they are able to project the right degree of modernity and tradition (Tokita-Tanabe, 2003). This self-representation of women parallels nationalist constructions of Indian womanhood by otherizing both Western women and less privileged Indian women. It may be appropriate to call the discourse of the new Indian woman an offshoot of the nationalist discourse.

From the discussion on nationalist discourses on Indian womanhood (Chatterjee, 1989; Chakravarti, 1989) and women's participation in the national movement (Forbes, 1996), two conclusions might be drawn: first that cultural discourses tend to exert pressure on individuals and influence their behaviour and second that while individuals might draw on cultural discourses, they also resist or subvert them in various ways. Similarly it is probably that the contemporary discourse of the new Indian woman which is closely connected with the celebratory discourses on India's globalization exerts some influence on the behaviour and experiences of individual middle class women. It is also probable that in their day-to-day lives women conform to or resist the discourse depending on context. In the next few chapters of this book I examine the lived experience of individual women in their families and workplaces to understand how they submit to, subvert or resist cultural values and social norms of appropriate female behaviour.

4
Individualism and Responsibility: Women's Relationships Within Their Families

In Chapter 2 I discussed Giddens' (1991, 1992) argument that the freeing of sex from reproduction results in plastic sexuality and the transformation of intimacy, contrasting it with Beck and Beck-Gernsheim's (1995, 2001) argument that individualization, particularly that of women, threatens the institution of family. Beck and Beck-Gernsheim argue that the contradiction between the flexibility and mobility required to succeed in the job market and the stability and rootedness required to create a strong family life can threaten the family. In spite of these crucial differences, both theorists are united in the position that modernity strengthens individualization.

A brief survey of articles in the popular press in India suggests that it is not only the extended reflexivity thesis that associates modernity with the disintegration of family life and the rising status of women. (See, for instance, Anon. (2005), 'India's New Worldly Women'; Alexander (2007), 'Women on Top'; Bhagat (2007), 'The Changing Indian Woman'.) While women are viewed as the beneficiaries of modernity, their emancipation is also believed to endanger 'traditional values'. This view may, in part, be attributed to the positioning of women as the custodians of tradition, as I argue in the previous chapter. Both these views – that of modernity as being uniformly beneficial in raising women's status and resulting in traditions being threatened – are misleading. The primary research cited in this chapter indicates that reality is more complex and nuanced than these views suggest.

I begin this chapter by examining the proposition that joint family structures are giving way to nuclear households in contemporary India. I examine some key discourses around women's position in the family, arguing that these discourses can be either strengthened or undermined by practice. I investigate a more contemporary discourse, that of individual choice and responsibility and its relationship with more traditional discourses on gender and family life.

Flexible household patterns and joint family relations

A common lament that one hears amongst the Indian middle classes is that with modernity and globalization people have no time for their families (Upadhya and Vasavi, 2006). Middle class professionals and their parents complain that the demands of work in a globalized economy have a detrimental effect on family life and that Western influences have strengthened individualism and materialism (Upadhya and Vasavi, 2006). People speak nostalgically about the days when siblings and cousins visited regularly and when family members celebrated holidays, festivals and feasts together. There is a widespread belief that the young are no longer concerned about their parents and that the traditional Indian joint family (consisting of parents, their married sons and daughters-in-law, unmarried children and grandchildren) is disintegrating. These views mirror Beck and Beck-Gernsheim's (1995, 2001) contention that families are threatened by market forces. However, as A. M. Shah (1973) argued forty years ago, and Mira Säävälä (1998) suggested more recently, the spirit of 'jointness' still marks many social, economic and ritual ties in Indian families.

The stereotypical joint family described above is widely celebrated in films and television as the quintessential Indian family but has seldom been widely prevalent. Large residential units of patrikin under the guardianship of the oldest male in the patrilineage were an urban phenomenon, often associated with wealthy upper caste families (Shah, 1973) who collectively own a family enterprise. Women's position in such families was arguably more circumscribed and constrained than in nuclear families (Liddle and Joshi, 1986). As I have argued in the previous chapter, in colonial India, upper caste women tended to enjoy less freedom of mobility than women from depressed castes, the latter being forced by necessity to work outside the home. The upper caste ideal of large joint families and the simultaneous suppression of women may have been accepted earlier by depressed castes who were attempting to enhance their status through 'sanskritization' (Srinivas, 1959),[1] but given the intersection of class with caste in contemporary India and the expansion of avenues for enhancing one's status, sanskritization is no longer widespread. Liddle and Joshi (1986) pointed towards this trend about twenty years ago in their research on women and employment in India.

The flexible structure of Indian households

Earlier Indologists such as Henry Maine (in Säävälä, 1998) claimed that the 'traditional' joint family is disintegrating as a result of urbanization and modernization into individual nuclear households. However, Shah (1973) and Säävälä (1998) argue that this fallacy stems from the failure to take into account the complex social, economic and ritual ties between discrete households related by blood or marriage. This oversight, Shah claims, is related to the lack of distinction between 'households' which are characterized by common residence and commensality and 'families' which are related through ties of blood or marriage that operate independent of residence patterns (Shah, 1973). In this book I use Shah's (1973) concept of household rather than the common terms, nuclear family or joint family, to describe participants' living arrangements. The term 'households' helps to account for the flexible and changing composition of residential units as well as ties across households. I use the terms 'family' to describe people immediately connected by blood or marriage (parents, children, siblings, spouses and parents-in-law) who may not always reside in the same household and 'kin-group' or 'extended family' to describe relationships with cousins, aunts, uncles and brothers-in-law or sisters-in-law.

While large households may not be the norm, many people live in three-generational households. In my research I found that research participants live in a variety of households: fourteen of the twenty-four married women live in simple households (married couple with or without children); the remaining ten live in complex households consisting of married couples, the parents of either spouse and their children. Of the two single women interviewed, one lives with her parents whilst the other lives in a hostel. However, some of the simple households are complex for a few months or longer as parents often visit adult children for long periods of time. The changing composition of Indian households has earned the name 'houseflows' (Trawick in Säävälä, 1998).

Of the various households in the study, a few cases are significant: Anjana, a manager in a multinational company lives with her parents, her mother-in-law, her husband and her young son in her parents' home (this is the largest household amongst all research participants). Anita lives with her husband, her two daughters and her husband's grandmother who supervises the running of the household. Her parents and parents-in-law visit from time to time. Swati lives with her eight-year-old daughter; her husband visits her every few months as he has a non-transferable public sector job in another city. They have chosen to live apart since her job pays much higher than his and allows them to create a more secure future. Her parents-in-law visit her for a few weeks several times a year to help with childcare. Hema, who had been married for a year and had no children at the time of the research, lives alone while her husband lives in another city where he has found a well-paid job; weekend visits are frequent between the two and they hope that the situation will be temporary. She often stays over at her parents' home which is not far from hers.

The argument that the new self-contained apartment complexes that are popular in metropolitan cities create a 'class-based lifestyle while fragmenting kinship or caste-based neighbourhoods' (Upadhya and Vasavi, 2006: 108) ignores continuing relationships between households related by blood or marriage. Many families purchase two or three flats in the same apartment complex, one for elderly parents and one for each of their (married) children. Thereby they ensure some privacy for individual households while maintaining close relationships and exchanging food, care and support. Upadhya and Vasavi claim that 'emerging residential patterns in cities such as Bangalore reflect and reinforce the process of social fragmentation and disembedding' (2006: 108), but I would argue that it is precisely to minimize social fragmentation that families tend to live close to one another. Family ties cut across class boundaries as upwardly mobile upper middle class professionals support their parents who might be from the lower middle classes.

It has been argued that traditional joint families are being 'reconstituted' amongst the middle classes for the purpose of childcare and that they 'do not represent an adherence to traditionalism so much as a convenient solution to the domestic problems of working couples' (Upadhya and Vasavi, 2006: 110). However, grandparents' involvement in childcare is not a new development (see Liddle and Joshi, 1986). It is possibly becoming more noticeable at present with more middle class women entering the workplace. The instrumentalism that Upadhya and Vasavi highlight in kinship relations is not a consequence of modernity. Many kinship relations irrespective of culture or geography tend to have instrumental and affective dimensions.

Reciprocity in kinship relations

Much of the earlier anthropological work on Indian kinship tended to take a 'systemic' view by discussing how families and lineages were structured and how different families were connected together by affinal ties (Madan, 1993; Trautmann 1979/1993; Dumont, 1966/1993; Karve, 1953/1993; Nongbri, 1988/1993). Norms regarding intermarriage, the 'exchange of women' and relative status between various kin were discussed (Madan,

1993; Trautmann, 1979/1993; Dumont, 1966/1993). For instance, Madan (1993) speaks at length about the relationship between a man and his wife's brother, which is at once characterized by difference in status and deep bonds of friendship. With the exception of certain matrilineal communities (the Nairs of the South and the Khasis of the North East), all kinship systems were said to be patrilocal and virilocal (requiring women to move from their fathers' to their husbands' homes). The kinship systems of North India and South India were compared, and differences such as taboos against marrying close kin (in the North) versus the prevalence of cross-cousin marriage (in some communities of the South) were highlighted (Dumont, 1966/1993). However, till recently, little work was done on the lived experience of kinship, especially for women. The lived experience of kinship can both uphold and contradict accepted norms of interaction and status differences (Das, 1993; Dube, 2001; Grover, 2010).

When women are viewed as independent actors within the kinship system, who create and sustain relationships with other women (and men) while continuing to be constrained by virilocality and patriliny, a clearer picture emerges of how kinship operates in day-to-day experience. Women's role in 'kin-keeping' (servicing and maintaining kinship bonds, exchanging family news and organizing family gatherings, sending cards and remembering birthdays) has been discussed in an American context by Rosenthal (1985) and Di Leonardo (1987) and in a British context by Finch and Mason (1993). A noticeable degree of (unpaid and invisible) labour is implicated in this exchange, which benefits not only individual women but also their husbands and children (Di Leonardo, 1987). Di Leonardo (1987) argues that like housework, women's 'kinship work' is often invisible, but it also empowers women, winning them social approval and prestige, which can be deployed to gain other benefits.

In India women usually engage in four types of reciprocal transactions in the kin-group. These include the exchange of material substances (food, gifts of clothing or household items), of care work (for grandchildren or the elderly for instance), of emotional 'goods' (care, affection, gestures of respect, deference and advice) and of hospitality. The degree to which these intangible emotional goods can be expected varies according to the nature of the relationship and the temperaments of the individuals involved.

I am the only daughter-in-law who's working, the other ones aren't. For my in-laws to realize that [the challenges for a woman who is employed] … My husband has made my mother-in-law realize that what I am because – we are not staying together but then it's like how he has put it to them, like how these things [like having a career] are very important things for me plus he's also made me realize that I need to put a line over here [fall in line with certain expectations of his parents]. That's what I'm saying. I'm growing in my patience and I'm growing to take on more responsibilities. I would say like – eh – earlier it was like [I would think] 'No this is not my responsibility; they need to take care of me.' But now it's like there is – I also need to put in more efforts to make that relation build. I had to actually disguise my own personality, my real personality of what I am in office in front of my mother-in-law. Really that happens you know, and slowly, slowly talking to her, now she's realized. Now she'll push me out [encourage me] for doing those things which I would like to do.(Upasna, 28, married, executive)

Upasna and her mother-in-law are involved in a reciprocal exchange of mutual understanding and support in order to build a stronger relationship. At first Upasna 'disguised her personality' not from motives of deceitfulness but as a gesture of respect for her in-laws' values, which she implies are more conservative than her own. But thanks to the intervention of her husband and Upasna's willingness to conform to their expectations, her mother-in-law is now willing to encourage her professional aspirations. Such transactions indicate how women overcome the disadvantages associated with their positions as daughters-in-law (discussed in the next section) and gain some measure of freedom within their conjugal families.

Family bonds are also strengthened when women jointly organize festive celebrations such as Diwali (the festival of lights), Varalakshmi Pooja (the worship of the Goddess Lakshmi to ensure the prosperity of husband and home), and Gowri Pooja or Durga Pooja (which celebrates the return of the Goddess Durga from her husband's house to her natal home). By women's accounts, men are often exempt from attending family celebrations while they themselves may be expected to take time off from work to attend them. Although they feel obliged to participate in these occasions they also enjoy the female camaraderie that comes into play in organizing them and look forward to the chance to reconnect with distant kin as well as close family.

When there is a function, everyone gets together and then suddenly you know that these are my people. It feels so good to know that the network that's there whether you keep in touch or not. (Beena, 30, married, manager)

Although Beena's remarks imply that women do not keep in touch as much as they might wish to, my research found that women do make an effort to exchange family news, plan holidays and provide emotional support to family members through email, the telephone and instant messenger. Although social networking was not commonly used at the time of the fieldwork, it may be supposed that Facebook too has become a means for keeping in touch.

Even though the demands of paid employment might compete with women's family responsibilities, the sense of moral responsibility associated with kinship relations motivates them to make time for kinship obligations. Finch and Mason (1993) argue that because women do not expect to be in full-time employment all through their lives but anticipate being financially dependent from time to time, they create relationships of mutual obligation through reciprocal exchange. In doing so they are motivated not only by self-interest and the desire for social approval but also by affection (Di Leonardo, 1987; Finch and Mason, 1993). Women's efforts in maintaining kinship relations raise questions about the equation of modernity with individualization and weakening of family ties.

Traditional discourses on Indian women's place in the family

Five traditional discourses influence women's positions in their families. These are transience in her parental home, marriage as destiny, motherhood as a source of legitmacy, the inferior position of wives and daughters-in-law and the hierarchy between bride-takers and bride-givers. These discourses, though older than the nationalist discourse of ideal Indian womanhood, are closely related to it. However, as I argued in the previous chapter, discourses have both oppressive and emancipatory potential. While they may influence the creation of an individual's self-identity, they are also subject to modification and resistance through individual agency. In this section I discuss how the discourse may influence or be subjected to the influence of an individual's agency.

The transience of a daughter in her natal home

> First, she is a daughter to her parents.
> Second, she is a wife to her husband

(and daughter-in-law to his parents).
Third, she is a mother to her sons (and daughters).

(Kakar, 1988: 45)

A woman's position in her natal family is centred on the discourse of transience and transferability. Traditionally a daughter is considered a 'guest' in her parents' home (Kakar, 1988: 49) since she will soon marry and enter another family where her 'real' life begins; in folk idioms she is *paraya dhan*, someone else's wealth, or *amanaat*, a trust to be nurtured and protected before being handed over to her rightful 'owners' (Madan, 1993: 291). These popular idioms reiterate the *kanyādāna* complex or 'gift of a virgin bride' (Madan, 1993: 302) to a suitable man. The gift of a daughter is considered one of the highest gifts that can be bestowed and gains the giver a high level of *punya*, religious merit (Shah1973). It assumes the superiority of the bride-takers to the bride-givers since it would be unthinkable to bestow such a precious gift as one's daughter on someone inferior in status.

Sociologists have argued that the hierarchical relationship between bride-givers and bride-takers is an outcome of the *kanyādāna* complex. The superiority of the groom's people who receive the bride is underlined in symbolic gestures during the marriage, for instance, by the father of the bride welcoming the groom by washing his feet, a custom that is practised across several communities in both North and South India. Gifts and hospitality are lavished on the groom's kin, establishing an enduring hierarchical relationship between the two families (Gupta, 2000).

Many wedding ceremonies reinforce the notion of transience symbolically, for instance, by the bride's throwing of rice over her shoulder to indicate the severing of ties with her natal home (Dube, 2001). However, parents' concern for their daughters' happiness continues long after the marriage. Her continuing visits to the natal home, particularly during pregnancy and childbirth, and her close involvement in her natal family's concerns belie the discourse of transience.

In her study of Punjabi kinship Das asserts that it 'operates at two levels – the biological and the social' (1993: 213): while the enduring nature of biological ties is recognized, honour requires individuals to transcend biological ties and wear the mask of social or cultural ties. In times of crisis, however, biological ties become much more significant. Her argument is borne out by Grover's (2010) more recent research in Delhi's slums, which found that women use their relationship with their natal families and the proximity to the natal home to bargain for a better position in the conjugal household. Grover found that if her husband is irresponsible or abusive, a woman returns to her natal home until he promises to change his behaviour. Often mothers encourage their daughters to return home out of concern for their safety or to appropriate their labour in the household.

Examining gender, sexuality and marriage amongst more affluent women in Mumbai, Puri (1999) found that the natal home is seen as a place where one can shed one's responsibilities and temporarily return to a more carefree state, away from restrictions of the conjugal home. Given the relative freedom that they enjoy as daughters, many women feel overwhelmed by the restrictions imposed on them as daughters-in-law. In these cases the natal home becomes a place for young married women to be themselves. If in-laws are abusive, if they make unreasonable demands for dowry and if husbands are violent, the natal home becomes a safe haven for women. Kanti escapes the chaos of her in-laws' home and her husband's violence by spending every weekend at her mother's house.

> Friday evenings we [she and her eight-year-old daughter] go there. Sunday evenings I come back. I've taken my DVD player along so my brother brings some DVDs and they sit and watch and I am like [watching] a few glimpses here and there. She'll be playing outside all the while, my daughter, so I sit with her and enjoy her company.

However, even if all is well in the conjugal home, my research found that the hierarchy between bride-givers and bride-takers requires a woman's natal family to constantly monitor her relationship with her in-laws and husband. If her professional life interferes with her family obligations, parents step in and fulfil these obligations themselves rather than expose her to the ire of her in-laws. Parents are closely involved in their daughters' personal lives, taking care of her children, helping with domestic chores and advising her on her relationship with her in-laws. Even when women do not live in the same city as their parents, regular communication and reduced costs of travel ensure that the discourse of transience seldom holds well in practice. Swati, whose household arrangements were discussed earlier (she lives in Bangalore with her daughter and her husband and in-laws who are based in Kolkota frequently visit her), recounts how her mother insisted that she spend more time with her in-laws when she visits Kolkota.

> My in-laws were staying with me in Bangalore. Then they left at the end of November. Then I went to Kolkota [on a holiday] in

mid-December and they were again coming back [to my home in Bangalore] on 30th January, so my husband told me, 'If you are coming here for two weeks, you be with me for two weeks. Don't go to my parents or your parents [her husband lives on his own near her in-laws' home].' Then my mum said, 'No, no, no. You are coming once in a while, only once in a year to Kolkota. You must visit your in-law's place. If he has some expectations from his wife, they also have some expectations from their daughter-in-law. You should respect that'. So I told him, 'No, no, no, I'll go to your parents' place at least for two or three days.' So he was very happy that I am taking the initiative to go there [and], so I went to my mother-in-law's place. (Swati, 35, manager, mother)

Swati's mother advised her to overlook her (and her husband's) own need for a privacy to meet the expectations of her (Swati's) in-laws and was willing to sacrifice her own desire to see her daughter, to the superior claims of the bride-takers. As Swati has chosen to (temporarily) live separately from her husband for professional reasons she is more vulnerable to social criticism, possibly another reason for her mother's concern that she should demonstrate her conformity to the duties of a daughter-in-law. Her mother's concern about her (Swati's) behaviour may be attributed to the position of South Asian women as the repositories of the *izzat* (honour) of two families, the one they were born in and the one they have been married into (Afshar, 1989). Women who fail to create strong relationships in their conjugal homes are a source of embarrassment to their natal families, especially to their mothers who are seen to have failed in their duty of schooling their daughters in the virtues of submissiveness and compliance. Thus the discourse of transience is undermined by parental concern for their daughter's happiness and the stability of her marriage.

Marriage as a woman's destiny

If a girl today asks me, 'Is it a good idea to get married?' I will say 'yes' you must get married and I ... Okay I will not make clichéd statements like, 'A woman is incomplete if she's not married,' or 'A woman is incomplete if she's not had children.' but ... it's important to have responsibility in life. You cannot run away from responsibility, you cannot leave, you – You cannot keep living life of being a free bird and no responsibilities and all that. I think it's beautiful to have a marriage and it's beautiful to have children and that's where I'm very traditional in my thinking. (Geetika, 32, manager, mother)

> I go back home like going to a cemetery because it's so quiet at home. They [her parents] have this swollen face. It's like, 'Okay my daughter's not married, like the sky is falling. (Lathika, 33, manager, single)

Cultural norms across India make marriage obligatory for both sexes. Given the importance of *kanyādāna* as a religious duty, parents feel a compulsion to arrange a good match for their daughter. In addition, acquiring a son-in-law of higher status and wealth is an important indicator of esteem within the kin-group and community. Parents who fail in this duty face criticism and ridicule and, as Lathika indicates, become depressed and disheartened. In the period prior to her marriage a young woman's reputation is closely guarded by her family. If she refuses to marry, delays marriage or fails to find a suitable match, she prevents her parents from gaining religious merit and causes them pain and humiliation in their old age.

From my research participants' accounts, unmarried women and their parents are pressured by the questions of curious relatives or from seeing other young women marrying. Members of the extended kin-group admonish the young woman for being 'too choosy', not projecting the right image in public (dressing inappropriately, not grooming herself, drinking, smoking or socializing freely with men) or focusing too much on her career (which could imply to potential grooms that she lacks domestic talents or price her out of the hypergamous marriage market). Many participants report that the phase of their lives when they are negotiating marriage choices is one of intense pressure and conflict with their parents. They experience high levels of stress as they deal with the influx of marriage proposals and subsequent meetings with potential grooms. The pressure of having to justify or explain their single status leads some women to avoid family gatherings altogether.

> It's everybody, it's everybody. I have stopped attending weddings ... it gets too irritating. They say, 'What's happening, any news? Why are you not getting married?' 'You're very picky?' 'Why don't you do something about your weight?' 'You will never find a perfect guy, just settle down.' I go to these parties and my friends introduce me to their wives. I become the crux of the conversation between husbands and wives in the bedroom that night – 'My wife was asking, 'Why is she not married?' ... Is it supposed to be some kind of a sickness like, 'Why are you having fever?' 'Because I got drenched in the rain last night.' It's not a condition, right? It's not a medical condition [breaking down]. (Lathika, 33, manager, single)

Not being married at thirty three may be considered deviant in a society where the mean age of marriage is 22 years (in 1997 according to the National Resources Centre for Women, 200-), so it is not surprising that Lathika faces so much pressure, inquisitiveness and disparagement. While all young women face the pressure to marry and desire to be suitably married as soon as possible, Lathika's and Geetika's accounts indicate some tension within the discourse of marriage as destiny.

Paid employment and high incomes have restricted a woman's choices within a hypergamous marriage market, while also giving them (relatively) more freedom and opportunity. Therefore, in spite of the threat of social exclusion and ridicule women do resist being pressured into marriages with men who do not meet their expectations. Geetika's remarks on marriage are made with reference to many young women in her office who are unmarried and unwilling to compromise on the choice of a groom. Lathika too faces criticism for being too picky or not conforming to the standards of an ideal bride – slim, demure and quiet. However, in spite of being eager to marry, she is steadfast in her commitment to waiting for the right man. While marriage and wifehood are central to a young woman's life, and many do marry young, there are women who resist the discourse to create some room for their individual choices and preferences.

The institution of arranged marriage still prevails but with significant modifications: more choice is incorporated into marriage, mutual compatibility is significant and women are encouraged to meet with potential grooms before committing to the marriage (Fuller and Narasimhan, 2008; Netting, 2010; Puri, 1999). No loss of face occurs if individuals meet but refuse to go ahead with the marriage. Families are less stringent than before regarding caste and sub-caste endogamy. Caste itself may be more broadly defined: for instance, instead of seeking a spouse from a defined sub-caste such as Iyengar Brahmin or Madhava Brahmin for their children, parents may be willing to accept 'any Brahmin'.

In contemporary globalizing India class (indicated by actual wealth or educational qualifications and professional success) may overtake considerations of caste (Tenhunen, 1999); that is, families are willing to consider matches from grooms belonging to broadly similar religious/linguistic backgrounds who have a higher class status over less qualified and successful persons of the same caste or sub-caste. Grooms with technical qualifications, jobs in the prestigious IT industry or in multinational companies and prospects of migrating to Western countries tend to be highly sought after. To a lesser degree the same may be true of brides; given the opportunities created by economic liberalization and the growth of the consumer economy in urban India, women's earnings are necessary to a family. Therefore alongside traditional considerations such as beauty, domestic talents and decorum, women's educational qualifications and employment are factors in making a good marriage.

Inter-caste marriages made by choice are increasing. Parents are often supportive of such marriages provided the partner is of a similar linguistic or religious background and equivalent socio-economic status. However, interreligious marriages still tend to attract an opposition from families. One participant, Deepika, who considered such a marriage, broke off her relationship and later married by choice within her own religious community to satisfy her parents while another, Swarna, went ahead with the marriage but was ostracized by her parents. At the time of our meeting it had been three years since she had spoken to them.

Though happy in her marriage and fond of her in-laws, Swarna still speaks of her relationship with her parents with regret and hopes to reconcile in the future. In the next section, I discuss the implications of decisions such as Swarna's on women's married lives. In their discussion of transnationalism and identity Smart and Shipman (2004) argue that transnational individuals' choices are marked by the need to demonstrate loyalty to the norms of their communities whilst creating a space for their individual identity and personal happiness. Their argument that transnational individuals sometimes sacrifice individualism to retain family support may be equally applicable to individuals who remain within their native culture whilst experiencing the cultural consequences of globalization.

Parental consent plays a crucial role in marriage. Amongst my participants sixteen of the twenty-four married women have made marriages of choice, but ideals of romantic 'love' did not always play a role in their decision. Some couples who marry by choice may do so based on practical considerations such as compatibility of temperaments, sameness of profession and similarity of social and linguistic backgrounds. Similarity of professional backgrounds is important so that husbands understand wives' professional commitments such as long hours or frequent travel. Paid employment gives women a chance to meet with men of similar professional and educational backgrounds and, importantly, similar or higher incomes, some of whom may be likely candidates for a (self)arranged marriage. Consider below Malini's practical approach to a marriage of choice:

> When my husband [who was a colleague at the office] asked me to marry him, I introduced him to my mother and asked her to talk to

him. I felt she would know better than me whether we are going to be happy ten years from now. (Malini, 33, currently not in employment (resigned as manager), mother)

Malini's remark indicates that the parameters of middle class marriage have expanded to include not just caste or religious endogamy but also companionship. However, she also suggests that parents are the best judge of whether this companionship can be established. Fuller and Narasimhan (2008) argue that while personal compatibility is important in contemporary middle class marriage, this compatibility is seen to reside in similarity of caste and linguistic background, education and family income; therefore, caste and class are reproduced.

In some cases the couple might consider themselves to be in love. As in Malini's case, once the question of marriage comes up the couple apply for parental sanction to carry it out, and this sanction is given after scrutinizing the partner involved and their family background. If there is opposition or hesitation on the parents' part, lengthy negotiations occur between the two generations till one convinces the other.

I told [my parents], 'See this is my opinion and I am not going to say 'no' for whatever you say. But later I should not feel if I would have told you, you would have made this [allowed me to marry]. I should not have regret that way. I am not going to act against your words. I am just telling you, it is all your decision. I can't assure for my happy life. I will take up my life whatever you are giving me but I can't assure for my happy life whatever you say. I will live, that's all.' I made clear that I am not going to be against them, I'll wait. (Shreela, 29, manager, mother)

Shreela's patience paid off and her parents accepted her choice but by her own admission, 'I really didn't enjoy my marriage charms. I was really dull because I was thinking about what my parents will be thinking about me and how much pain they will be having.' That her parents had accepted her choice in defiance of opposition by the kin-group increases her sense of obligation to them, a debt that she repays through affection and reverence. Her account is littered with phrases like, 'I need to appreciate my mother for ...' and 'I must mention the contribution of my father to ...'.

In her critique of Giddens, Jamieson (1999) argues that acceptance of values such as democracy and intimacy do not necessarily result in greater equality for women, although it gives them new parameters within which they assess their relationships. Middle class Indian women and their parents often struggle to find partners who fulfil the traditional requirements of caste or religious endogamy and contemporary criteria of companionship and intimacy. Changing values, the emerging ethos of individualism and the idealization of romantic love encourages women to seek more choice in marriage, but the need for security obliges them to apply for parental approval and remain within broadly defined boundaries of caste and community.

As Geetika's argument at the beginning of this section indicates, while marriage is accepted as a normative goal for all individuals, the discourse of marriage as destiny is slowly giving way to the discourse of marriage as responsibility. Marriage is no longer an event that 'happens' to women but a choice that they actively make with their parents. As individual choice increases in arranged marriage, so does the notion of individual responsibility. The manner in which the research participants understand their experiences indicates that the responsibility of getting married at the right age, to the right person is increasingly being carried by individual women in the middle classes. While this responsibility is shared with parents in the case of arranged marriages, the anxieties associated with this responsibility are perhaps most keenly felt by those women who exercise their choice against parental wishes. In the next section I explore how women carry this responsibility after entering the conjugal home.

The subordination of wives

Hindu mythology is replete with figures symbolic of wifely devotion, the submissive Sita, the self-sacrificing Sati, the tenacious Savitri whose qualities are extolled in devotional songs and everyday speech. As prototypes for heroines on films and television, these mythological figures have an influence that cuts across religions, linguistic groups and regions. Their ubiquitous presence in Indian popular culture has led previous scholars to argue that they personify the ideal of Indian womanhood in the collective psyche (Kakar, 1988). Scholars in the 1970s and 1980s tended to argue that gendered relations in marriage are characterized by inequality of status and power and that women are inevitably subjugated within their marital home (Kakar, 1988; Dhruvranjan, 1989 in Puri, 1999; Caplan, 1985). However, more recent scholarship argues that both men and women seek companionship, equality and intimacy within marriage (Puri, 1999; Netting, 2010).

> I don't think I could have been married to anybody else and felt so happy. I don't know. Either you adapt yourselves to suit each other

or it must be a God-made match ... I think today people are enjoying their marriages a lot more. It's no longer a responsibility or a duty you're fulfilling – it's about being married to a friend almost, so the way we approach our marriages and our lives also are so different from what our parents must have [lived]. (Beena, 30, manager, married)

He doesn't know I'm existing next to him. I'm a newly married bride. I'm his wife. The touch or the feel, the talk, the romance, the sex, nothing was in our life. Then I thought, 'Okay, this is a wrong decision [to have married this man].' I didn't know how to react because I was also not mature to think in that way.' ... I pray and that gives me all the courage ... I'm not a patient girl but prayer works. God has yoked me and my husband so I thought he's keeping us together. Forgive a person however sinful he is and take him as a new person in my life. (Cristina, 29, secretary, mother)

Both Chrisina and Beena had arranged marriages. Both believe that their marriages are ordained by a supernatural power, yet one accepts her marriage as a 'yoke from God', the other as a gift. Although participants' experiences of empowerment in marriage may differ, their accounts indicate similar expectations from marriage, including equality, romance and companionship. However, a sense of duty still lies beneath these expectations as Cristina suggests. Since the reduced stigma around divorce makes marriages in contemporary India more vulnerable, women put in high levels of emotional labour to maintain their marriages (Hochschild, 2003):

It is so easy. It is so easy to get out of a marriage. It's just the easiest thing today – in today's time when you are independent financially, when you have parents who may welcome you back. ... Ask yourself, 'You want this marriage to work?' And the answer is, 'Yes I want it to work. I got married because I want it to work.' Who's going to take that effort to make it work? If it's not your husband then it's you. And you will take that effort. You will say sorry and you will make up. And that is the effort you have to take whether it's your fault or it is not. (Geetika, 32, manager, mother)

My brother is having an arranged marriage, my sister had an arranged marriage. A relative ticked me off, saying, 'Your marriage [by choice, outside her sub-caste] won't last long, so I was determined that whatever happens I will keep it together. (Jaya, 33, manager, mother)

When women such as Geetika and Jaya marry by choice, their individualism tends to erode the family's protective influence, leaving them feeling vulnerable and exposed. Therefore they take pains to preserve their marriages. Employment and financial independence may make it easier, as Geetika suggests, to leave a marriage but divorce continues to be stigmatized. As Adkins (2000) argues, reflexivity has different consequences for men and women; while it may disembed women from some traditional constraints, such as the more oppressive aspects of family life, it also re-embeds them within new constraints. Moreover, while the language of individualism may apply to the private tie between husband and wife, marriage continues to be conducted under the gaze of the kin-group.

> I am not allowed to address him by name in front of my relatives and all. They're very particular. They're still in [a] back[ward] stage. You're not supposed to call your husband by his name. I say *hogo-baro* [go-come] to him at home but in front of them I have to be respectful. I'm forced to say *bannee kooth-koli* [please come and do sit down]. I feel he is very distant to me and he also doesn't like it. (Hema, 26, administrator, married)

While she has a casual and intimate relationship with her husband in private, in front of her more conservative family, Hema follows the traditional norm of speaking formally with her husband and not addressing him by name. Even her husband's professed discomfort with this equation does not motivate him to change it before the extended kin-group as some degree of collusion between husband and wife is necessary to win the extended family's approval of a woman's conduct. Couples move from their more equitable relationship in private to one that recognizes the authority of the husband in public. As part of the patriarchal bargain, women selectively uphold some traditional norms of unequal status, to receive love, support and protection within marriage (Kandiyoti, 1988).

The reification of romantic love and the ideals of egalitarianism encourage women to seek equality within their marriages. Yet structural inequalities (differences in income, age and life experience), cultural factors (the continuance of the breadwinner–caregiver model and the romanticization of the husband–protector ideal) and traditional norms (such as the hierarchy between bride-givers and bride-takers) prevent them from fully realizing this equality. Some participants attempt to mask this inequality by indicating that they are 'equal in the ways that "really count"' because the closeness of the marital tie 'calls for some disguise of the subordination that women experience within it' (Hochschild, 2003: 169). Being equal in the ways that count includes joint decisions about children, being consulted on financial issues, being encouraged to remain in employment and some (but by no means equal) sharing of household tasks.

Amongst the contemporary middle classes in India, the discourse of subordination of wives is considerably weaker even if broad inequalities of status persist between men and women. Women see marriage as a relationship of equality and intimacy which needs to fulfil the emotional needs of both partners, a view that encourages them to demand greater emotional involvement from men. Many women argue that there is greater equality in their marriages than those of their parents. While the research found that cases of emotional or physical abuse, indifference or conflict do exist in contemporary marriages, employment tends to empowers women in dealing with these issues.

The inferior position of daughters-in-law

It is the mother's duty to train her daughter up to be an absolute docile daughter-in-law. The summum bonum of a girl's life is to please her parents-in-law and her husband. If she does not 'get on' with her mother-in-law, she will certainly be a disgrace to her family and cast a blot on the fair name of her mother. (Srinivas, 1942, cited in Kakar, 1988: 51)

The inferior position of daughters-in-law in their conjugal home is legitimized by mythology, films and more recently by a highly orthodox portrayal of women in television soaps and advertisements. Indian television is replete with models of daughters-in-law who sacrifice their own aspirations and desires for the greater good, guard family honour and encourage unity amongst its members. They are frequently upheld as perfect examples of Indian womanhood. In spite of the popularity of these films and television serials, research has found that many young women question the normative standards of female behaviour that they valourize (Poggendorf-Kakar, 2001). The term 'Sati-Savitri', a compound of Sati and Savitri, mythological figures who embody ideal womanhood, is often used to ridicule uncalled-for levels of sacrifice by women. Yet, the ubiquity of these ideals and images on television, in films and on calendar art indicates their influence on the collective Indian psyche.

If young women reject submissiveness and aspire for more egalitarian relationships with their husbands, in-laws frequently expect conformity and deference from daughters-in-law (Puri, 1999). In the early years of marriage women struggle with the norms and lifestyle of the conjugal home. Consider these contrasting indications from young women who have recently been married and live with in-laws:

> There was always this expectation that we have to spend so-called quality time with my in-laws. I think that was the crux of the whole problem – the craving for attention ... I have a job which is so demanding. I also have some obligation towards my parents and it's not as if we're ignoring them [her in-laws]. We're living with them and then there is the constant expectation which is sort of piled on to you. You get some spare time on a Saturday or a Sunday. When you've gone through an entire week where you've barely spent time with each other and you're thinking that Saturday-Sunday is the time when you probably spend time with your husband – and they're sitting with these long faces saying, 'We were thinking that we'll all go out as one big happy family.' And I'm thinking, 'I don't want to go out with you!' [laughter]. (Rupa, 28, manager)

> I make a conscious effort, like on weekends I ensure that I spend a lot of time at home doing whatever they want to do and that's mainly because there was scepticism about our relationship. I just want to please them and make sure they don't have any regrets [about consenting to the marriage after much hesitation], but over the months that I have tried doing that I've actually found that I like getting pampered and they treat me like their daughter. That's something that I feel I am getting rewarded [for]. (Nitya, 27, manager)

Rupa who has had an arranged marriage resists her in-laws' expectation that she 'spend quality time with them', though she does not engage in open confrontation. In contrast, Nitya, whose marriage of choice was initially opposed by her in-laws, takes pains to please them. It may be argued that her individualism in opting for an inter-caste marriage has threatened the authority of the elders. Therefore she attempts to re-establish this authority by conforming to their wishes and receives affection and acceptance in return. In late modernity, Indian women may 'choose' to treat their parents-in-law with deference, rather than being 'expected' to do so, but their choice is mediated by several cultural parameters (Adams, 2003): the concern of their own parents (that their daughter demonstrates that she has been well schooled in the duties of motherhood and wifeliness), the overt or covert expectations of in-laws, the substitute care that they provide for grandchildren, gendered messages acquired in childhood and fear of negative evaluation in the kin-group.

While many women strive to win the approval and affection of their in-laws, they also negotiate for recognition of their own needs and desires in the conjugal home, as Rupa indicates. A few women report serious conflicts, usually when their employment and income threatens the authority of their mothers-in-law, in which case they have little recourse but to turn to their natal families for support. Kanti, whose own mother was not in a position to help her, felt her position to be particularly vulnerable. However, in her negotiations with her in-laws she rarely conformed to notion of inferiority in status. It may be argued that while women may not feel themselves to be inferior, the older generation may uphold the discourse of inferiority, at least covertly. Women therefore take pains to avoid situations where the authority of the in-laws is threatened or where they become isolated in the conjugal home. Consider this exchange from a focus group:

Anjali: You can go as far as you want, you can rise as high as you want to [in the workplace], but I think on the personal front, on the family front there are a certain amount of things that you need to do or you want to do. I don't think anybody dictates that you have to do it but it's a certain amount of the upbringing, certain amount of maternal instincts and your wifely instincts [laughter], daughter-in-law-ly and sisterly.

Swarna: But we also do that because it makes you happy at the end of the day if you want to be a typical daughter-in-law; it's because it makes you happy ultimately. So what's happening to us is that we've finally realized it's very important to make ourselves happy rather than make others happy. (Anjali, 30, manager, mother; Swarna, 31, manager, mother)

In spite of their exposure to ideals of equality and egalitarianism, most middle class women respect the traditional norms associated with their status as daughters-in-law and behave accordingly. They are rewarded for their compliance with affection, care and support for their professional lives. The manner in which compliance with tradition is exchanged for practical and emotional support, help with childcare and encouragement of professional life will be further examined in Chapter 6. However, it is important to emphasize here that women describe their conformity using the vocabulary of individualism prevalent in late modernity. They describe it not as a constraint but as a choice that is gladly made. While this description may be in some cases a face-saving exercise in a culture where individualism enjoys high purchase, it may be still argued that women no longer find traditional discourses around the importance of wifehood or motherhood and the vulnerability of a woman in her conjugal home useful in understanding their positions as daughters-in-law. The new individualist discourse of self-fulfilment and self-expression allows them to account for their behaviour whilst also maintaining their self-identities as modern, independent and self-sufficient women. Jackson's (2008) argument of relational reflexivity is appropriate here. Women's construction of their self-identities depends not only on their ability to reflect on themselves but to do so in the light of the opinions of others. The praise and affection they receive augments their self-worth and sense of personal fulfilment.

Motherhood as the fulcrum of a woman's identity

Hindu society is not unique in revering motherhood as a moral, religious or even artistic ideal, but the absolute and all-encompassing social importance of motherhood, the ubiquitous variety of mother-hood myths, and the function of offspring in ritual and religious (not to mention economic) life all give to motherhood in Indian culture a particularly incontrovertible legitimacy. (Kakar, 1988)

The centrality of motherhood in India is underlined by myth and folklore about the innocent, guileless and mystical nature of mater-nal love. The obsession of the mythical mother Yashoda with her son Krishna and that of the Goddess Parvati with Ganesha is eulogized in stories, folk songs and films. Motherhood is traditionally the fulcrum of an Indian woman's identity, her highest achievement (Kakar, 1988; Dube, 2001). It confers on her a sense of respectability and authority, thus strengthening her position in her conjugal home.

None of my participants saw motherhood as optional; only one woman was delaying motherhood as she was unsure whether her mar-riage would last. All the mothers remarked that after childbirth their identities had irrevocably changed and every relationship came second to motherhood, a finding that is borne out by Puri's (1999) research. Puri (1999) found that motherhood not only creates new responsi-bilities but also integrates women more strongly within the conjugal home, giving them a greater sense of control. I found along with Puri (1999) that women's accounts of motherhood are deeply influenced by dominant discourses, but in the case of my interviewees the demands of employment make it difficult to live up to these ideals, causing high levels of guilt and anxiety.

> I probably try a little more of what I've read here and there rather than doing instinctive parenting. I logged on to a site – one of my friends had told me it was a very good site – Babysitter.com. It said every month, what to expect out of your child and it was so true. 'This month your child will try this', and it happened like that so I wanted to handle it better. 'Your child might talk back. That is her way of testing the ground', so I should learn to be little more careful not to react to those things. I am more disciplined and I expect her to do all the jobs. 'You pick a toy you have to put it back.' (Malini, 33, currently not in employment (resigned as manager), mother)

Most of the mothers I interviewed report that they regularly read books and magazine articles or browse websites on parenting. One participant, Shreela, reported receiving books on pregnancy and parenting as a gift from her husband and mother-in-law. Some participants maintain files of articles for future reference and consciously implement the recommendations in them, arguing that the experts predict with surprising accuracy how a child will behave at each stage of her growing years. Most experts underscore the importance of 'intensive mothering': reading to children, supervising their homework, overseeing their nutrition, planning their extracurricular activities and ensuring their emotional well-being. They tend to set impossible standards for employed mothers who cannot keep up with their responsibilities (Pocock, 2003: 81). In addition the middle classes' concern with investing in the cultural capital of their children (Béteille, 1993) requires mothers to put in a great deal of effort into supporting their children's education and 'personality development'.

Giddens (1991) argues that one of the defining characteristics of late modernity is the tendency for individuals to turn to experts for advice on all aspects of life and particularly in intimate relations. Of all intimate relations, mothering is arguably the most stringently policed both by experts such as teachers, educators, counsellors and psychologists, and grandparents, relatives and neighbours. In the discourse of experts, conception, pregnancy and motherhood are not natural occurrences but 'projects' to be undertaken with care and responsibility (Beck and Beck-Gernsheim, 1995). However, growing children suffer a variety of minor or major illnesses, go through phases of withdrawal or misbehaviour, become unhappy at school or fail to meet educational standards. Any such occurrence might lead a mother to question her parenting.

> At the last PTA meeting that I went – it wasn't very great. I saw the previous conversation between the mother and teacher; they are going gaga over that kid and she was spending more [time] – probably half an hour. I was waiting for my turn, when I went we hardly had five minutes talk in a way. It was okay for me, I wanted to come back to office but I was wondering why. (Jaya, 33, manager, mother)

Jaya is concerned that her eight-year-old son is far too quiet and reticent in school. His teacher's failure to praise him made her question if she was doing enough to support his schooling. Educational decisions are probably the most difficult for young mothers, given the plethora of choices and the conflicting messages of experts regarding scholastic achievement, competition, how much academic pressure is optimal and the diverse educational philosophies that various schools follow in India. While some of the concern may be shared by fathers, mothers still report being consumed by anxiety about their decisions. Their experiences may be aptly captured by Beck and Beck-Gernsheim's (1995) argument that children have become an all-consuming project in late modernity.

However, in the Indian context traditional discourses around selfless motherhood are further strengthened by the positioning of the child as a delicate project. Women may not directly draw on mythical stereotypes in describing their mothering (although these stereotypes such as that of the selfless mother of Krishna, Yashoda, continue to exist in films, television and other forms of popular culture). However, the high standards of mothering set by their own mothers, by child-rearing experts or by neighbours and relatives who are stay-at-home mothers cause them to put their children's needs far above their own well-being. In spite of grandparents' close involvement in childcare amongst the contemporary middle classes, women feel pressured by both traditional and contemporary discourses in this arena. In their attempt to balance the demands of employment with the intensive requirements of mothering, many women experience high stress and chronic sleep deprivation, a situation that is further explored in Chapter 6.

Conclusion

Women's accounts indicate that contrary to both academic and popular opinion, families continue to be strong in the face of modernity and globalization. Whilst families may be smaller in size, emotional, economic, ritual and practical ties between family members continue to exist. The research suggests that women play an important role in servicing and maintaining these ties. However, the continuance of the family does not imply that traditional discourses regarding women's positions in their families remain frozen. Day-to-day lived experience can undermine as well as strengthen traditional discourses. Women choose to adopt or discard elements of the discourses in their daily lives, strategically behaving according to traditional norms or ignoring them. In accepting traditional norms they might be motivated by love, by an impetus to obtain other forms of support or by concern for family honour and prestige. They might at times conform due to social pressures and the fear of stigma. However, they also exercise agency in choosing which norms they follow.

While some traditional discourses such as that of transience in the parental home or subordination in the conjugal home become weaker with modernity, others, including the discourses on selfless motherhood and significance of marriage, are strengthened by the contemporary discourse of choice and responsibility. Just as traditional discourses are not uniformly oppressive of women, the discourse of individual choice and responsibility does not consistently lead to empowerment and emancipation. It brings some advantages to women in terms of enabling them to take a more active role in professional and marital decisions but can also leave them alone in dealing with consequences of their decisions whilst masking the limits of their choice. This vulnerability is particularly noticeable when women make marriages of choice.

In interrogating the effect of modernity on women's positions within their homes, it is important to move beyond simplistic equations of modernity with individualism and tradition with collective obligations and responsibilities. Even though women use the language of individual choice and responsibility to describe their collective obligations, they do not favour a form of individualism that liberates them from family obligations, nor do they find their families to always be oppressive of their freedom. Although they are sometimes motivated to conform to traditional norms by guilt and fear of social disapproval, women also value the love, support and encouragement that they receive within their families. They are consequently willing to conform to the expectations associated with their positions as daughters, wives, mothers and daughters-in-law. This conformity earns them the support and protection of their families which, as the next two chapters will argue, is vital to their professional success.

5
Women's Relationships with Paid Work in the Transnational Economy

This chapter examines middle class women's motivations to enter the globalized labour market and the differences in their access to the resources required to succeed in it. As Table 5.1 suggests, the proportion of adult women in paid employment in India is only about 33%, and of these women a very small number are in the organized sector. The unorganized sector itself accounts for over 90% of the total workforce according to the National Sample Survey 2004–2005, and a larger proportion of women workers are in this sector (National Informatics Centre, Government of India, 2009). However, after economic reforms in 1991, multinational companies began to enter India and local companies established a transnational presence, particularly in the IT industry. Following the growth of the organized sector, particularly in the form of private industry, there has been much hype around the creation of jobs for women in the organized sector, particularly the prestigious IT industry where a third of the workforce is said to be women. Therefore, one may draw some conclusions about women's relationships with paid work in the transnational economy based on the experiences of women in the IT industry. Within the transnational economy I include organizations that engage in economic relationships across two or more nation states. Both multinational companies which have offshore development centres in India and local companies that provide goods and services to markets overseas would be part of the transnational economy.

Two major studies on middle class women published in the 1980s, Caplan's (1985) study on class and gender in southern India and Liddle and Joshi's (1986) research on working women in Delhi, have had contradictory findings regarding employment. Caplan (1985) argues that middle class women rarely engage in paid employment as it is stigmatized as a sign of financial misfortune and a slight on their husbands'

Table 5.1 Gender-wise estimates of employment in India

Employment measures	Men	Women	Total
Workforce (in thousands)[a]	336,592	129,678	466,270
Work force participation rate (%)[a]	81.1% of population aged over 15 years	33.1% of population aged over 15 years	57.8% of population aged over 15 years
Employment in organized sector (in thousands)[b]	45,784	10,716	56,450
Gender composition of organized sector (%)[b]	81%	19%	100%
IT workforce (in thousands)[c]	1,629	671	2,300
Gender composition of IT workforce (%)[c]	70% of IT workforce	30% of IT workforce	100%

[a] ILO EAPEP (Estimate and Projections for Economically Active Population) for 2008.
[b] National Informatics Centre, Ministry of Labour, Government of India (2009); the above estimates are for the year 2006, published in 2009.
[c] Estimates for 2008 based on NASSCOM (2010a) and NASSCOM (2009).

breadwinning capabilities. She states that families rarely support their daughters and daughters-in-law in engaging in paid work even while they might allow them to continue in higher education. Moreover, she contends, paid employment still holds a number of barriers for women. In contrast, Liddle and Joshi argue that women do succeed in professional life, sometimes with support from their families and sometimes without (admittedly in many cases the support from male relatives comes after women have achieved some success in higher education or professional life). They contend that families derive prestige and status from women's professional roles. Unlike Caplan's study, Liddle and Joshi's interviews were restricted to women in paid employment, which could account for the difference in their findings.

Both studies found that limitations were imposed by families on women's education. The education system was also not favourable to women: girls' schools and colleges were not well distributed across the country; facilities for women students were poor; there were no provisions for their safety and the number of women teachers and lecturers was low. They found that barriers existed against women in the labour market, including taboos against the sexes mixing freely in public, restrictions on women's mobility, the dual burden of housework and paid work and discrimination at the workplace. Both studies suggest that women in paid employment are often subject to strict scrutiny to ensure that their behaviour meets prevailing standards of respectability.

The women discussed in this study are at least a generation behind the women interviewed by Caplan (1985) and Liddle and Joshi (1986). Growing up in the late 1980s and 1990s, the period of economic reform and technological progress, many of them benefitted from the impetus given to higher education in that period and the growth of private industry. They were strongly influenced by the middle class value placed on educational achievement, professional success and financial stability. They did not consider higher education a stop-gap arrangement before marriage but a means to a well-paid job. For them paid labour is not an act of rebellion or a sign of misfortune but, as one of my interviewees put it, 'the reason why I studied'. In this respect their relationship with paid labour is considerably different from that of employed women in the 1980s.

Middle class Indian women's presence in the labour market is both a matter of choice and compulsion. While many of them experience a sense of guilt when they evaluate their commitments to paid work in relation to prevalent ideologies of motherhood, they rarely see complete withdrawal from the labour market as a solution. Their relationship with paid employment is considerably different from that of the women interviewed by Caplan (1985) twenty-five years ago (with some significant similarities which I discuss latter in this chapter).

The accounts of the women I interviewed suggest that rather than engaging in the labour market as individualized workers, their motivations to work are closely bound with their family responsibilities. Their capacity to succeed professionally is often directly influenced by the financial and emotional investments that their parents are able to make, while their continuance in the labour market after childbirth depends partly on the financial needs of their families and partly on the support of their mothers and mothers-in-law. This last issue is dealt with in greater detail in the next chapter. Here I explore some structural factors that influence women's chances in the new transnational economy, their relationships with paid work and their motivations to enter the labour market. Although the women I interviewed are employed in the IT industry, one may cautiously draw from their experiences some generalizations about women's employment in private industry in general. Given the IT industry's position as the forerunner of globalization in India, other globalized industries such as banking, financial services, telecommunications, pharmaceuticals and biotechnology tend to model themselves on it; therefore, women's experiences of entering and succeeding in them are likely to be similar. Before examining women's experiences of employment in these industries, however, I examine the individualization of the labour market in late modernity.

Individualization of the labour market in late modernity

In examining the labour market it is important to distinguish between the conditions of the market and the discourses that strengthen these conditions. Two major conditions of the labour market identified by the reflexive modernity thesis are individualization and risk. Both are closely associated with globalization, with the increasing popularity of neoliberal ideas and the dismantling of state-sponsored welfare policies. As economies across the globe are more closely integrated with each other, corporations can source the cheapest raw material, labour, goods and services from across the globe. They are in a position to play off countries and locations against one another, moving to a new location if labour policies in their current location obstruct their pursuit of profit (Beck, 2000). Therefore the labour market across the world becomes highly flexible. Flexibilization of the labour market in late modernity creates high levels of job insecurity. More workers are hired on temporary, short-term contracts which can be terminated as market conditions change. While employers can adapt the size of the workforce to suit their needs, such a workforce faces the constant threat of unemployment. Women tend to be over-represented in these sorts of part-time, contractual jobs rather than in more secure, prestigious and high-paying full-time jobs.

Giddens accurately identified time–space distanciation as a significant feature of the new globalized economy. This results in the disembedding of relationships from local and national contexts and the creation of close relationships between individuals and organizations across geographies. However, he fails to account for the unequal nature of these relationships which enable clients in developed economies to demand work at low cost and within very tight deadlines from service providers in emerging economies. Clients use the difference in time zones and the availability of superior communication technologies to instigate conference calls late in the evening, demand work at family unfriendly hours and interrupt religious festivals and national holidays (Upadhya and Vasavi, 2006).

While many of the arguments of the reflexivity thesis have been developed with reference to Europe and North America, individualization of the labour market is evident in other parts of the globe. Economic deregulation may have increased job opportunities and incomes in the private sector in India, but it has also contributed to the instability of the job market (Fernandes, 2006). As the national and international economies become more closely linked, Indian employees face the possibility of losing their jobs or taking a cut in their incomes in times of global financial crises. Increasingly, workers are supplied via 'labour contractors' as a result of which they do not enjoy the same rights as employees and find it difficult to negotiate higher wages or better working conditions.

Under conditions of individualization, the discourse of individual choice and responsibility enjoys high purchase. Contracts between employers and employees in late modernity do not presume lifelong commitments; instead the employer provides employees with opportunities for professional growth and exposure while the latter are expected to make the effort to gain maximum benefit from each assignment in terms of either experience or skills. In this manner employees improve their employability and career prospects, moving on according to the availability of job opportunities. Institutionalized individualization within the labour market leads to the decline of unions and other forms of collective representation. Employees are expected to take an entrepreneurial approach to work, planning their own careers, negotiating their own contracts, working arrangements and wages. They take personal responsibility for their career progression, training and professional success. What the discourse obscures, however, are the inequities which influence their access to the apparatus for success. It might be imagined that given the relative autonomy that they enjoy within their roles, it is easier for professionals and managers to be entrepreneurial, while it is difficult for administrative staff, who are usually on temporary contracts, to take the same approach. However, my research has found, in keeping with Leela Fernandes's (2006) work on the middle classes and employment, that both groups feel equally vulnerable. Managers might not be on temporary contracts, but they believe that during a recession or in case of a take-over of their company they are equally likely to be made redundant. Whether their perception of their vulnerability is true may be questionable, but it causes considerable anxiety.

There are lot of risks that we have taken, for example, this building, this house – because IT industry is very dynamic, anything could happen anytime. There is this threat of us – Yeah, I need to tell you this. There is this threat of us losing our jobs, and there is this threat of us downsizing and taking an undercut in our salaries. ... He [my husband] said very clearly, 'You don't worry, worst comes to worst, we'll sell one property. ... whatever we have built, we'll sell it off and pay back the loan. Just keep cool.' Very complicated my life, no? [laughing]. (Anjana, 33, manager, mother)

The discourse of individual choice and responsibility has been found to influence the work culture and human resource policies of the new globalizing economy in India, which consists of transnational corporations as well as smaller companies servicing markets in the USA, UK, Europe and East Asia. From employee acculturation and training programmes of transnational organizations, it is evident that individualism is strongly valued in the private sector (Sathaye, 2008; Upadhya and Vasavi, 2006). Sathaye (2008) argues that the discourse of such programmes tends to reify self-reliance and individual effort over social and economic factors in achieving success.

An emphasis on individual efforts is also evident in the speech and writings of industry leaders (see Bagchi, 2007; Das, 2000). In a speech addressing potential leaders amongst women professionals, Subroto Bagchi, a leading industrialist, argues that women cannot be successful professionals 'by trying to juggle work, home, husband, mother-in-law and making pickle'; rather successful women are 'steadfastly committed to their respective professions and they are very ambitious individuals who are focused on the goal that demands a price paid at the entrance [the price implied being a serious commitment to family and children]' (Bagchi, 2007).

Within the values of the new economy, the ideal worker is characterized as one who is flexible, mobile and willing to allow work to enter personal time zones and spaces. Workers are treated as independent entities with no personal commitments to compete with their professional goals (Beck and Beck-Gernsheim, 2001). Mobility is also an important factor for success in such a market: workers are expected to migrate according to the demands of management or the flow of capital (Guillaume and Pochic, 2009; Upadhya and Vasavi, 2006). Since many women cannot easily relocate or even travel for short periods of time due to their caring and domestic responsibilities, their personal vulnerability or prevalent social norms and structures, they are considerably disadvantaged in the workplace. Bagchi's argument confirms the findings of Wajcman's (1998) research on women in top management which indicates that they are much less likely to have families and children than men in similar positions.

Official discourse suggests that the new globalized economy is meritocratic in nature, enabling individuals to succeed on the basis of talent, hard work and their conformity to the values of individualism, flexibility and mobility. From Giddens' point of view it enables workers to act as reflexive agents, making informed career choices in pursuit of success. Yet, as previous research on the IT industry suggests, in reality some individuals are more equipped by ascribed values of class, caste or geography to succeed in the labour market than others (Upadhya and Vasavi, 2006; Krishna and Brihmadesam, 2006). In the next few sections I explore how class interacts with gender to influence women's capacity to succeed in the labour market and their relationship with paid work.

Differential access to cultural capital and parental support

Two important factors distinguish women's access to education in the 1990s and afterwards from those of previous generations of middle class Indian women. One is the recognition of education as essential to success in the global economy, and the other is the overall expansion in higher education as a result of government policies established in the 1980s. Since many universities and colleges in India are subsidized by the government, college fees for undergraduate degrees such as the Bachelor of Arts, Commerce or Science are relatively affordable for middle class families[1] although technical education such as Engineering, Architecture or Medicine is more expensive. Research participants stated that their parents expected them to acquire at least a college degree, and nearly all of them were expected to undertake paid work afterwards. However, there is a marked difference between the old and new middle classes' access to education and other forms of cultural capital required to succeed in the globalizing economy.

Unlike many upper middle class employed women in Liddle and Joshi's (1986) research who fought their parents, their teachers and the educational establishment to be allowed to access education, the upper middle class women I interviewed tended to not only enjoy parental support for their educational goals, but they were also subjected to the middle class pressure to achieve. Amongst the middle classes hard work, ambition and determination are highly valued, and children experience high pressure to succeed in education and in professional life (Béteille, 1993). Upper middle class parents willingly invest in high-quality private education, extra tuitions, hobby classes, books and educational games to help their children gain knowledge and skills required to succeed.

> My mother especially was extremely ambitious for me. My father has always guided me. I was one of the few who at that age got career counselling. It's commonplace today. It wasn't so common at that time. (Maya, 37, manager, mother)

> When myself, my sister and my brother, we had any discussion, we were very clear that we had to work. Probably it was my mother's influence. She had the dream to work. Unfortunately my grandfather expired when she was young so she had to settle for a married life. So she always had this dream that we will study well and do something for ourselves. And I think that's why my father also went away [to work in a big city] so he could provide us a better life. (Jaya, 33, manager, mother)

Maya and Jaya are old middle class women whose parents had modest incomes. However, both had very different upbringings. Maya grew up in Mumbai, a large metropolitan city, whereas Jaya spent her early years in her native village before moving to the city of Hyderabad. Compared to Jaya, Maya had much easier access to the cultural capital required to succeed. Nevertheless both had parents who were highly ambitious and drove them to achieve. Béteille argues that parental involvement creates both the skills and the motivation to succeed.

Many mothers attempted to live out their own thwarted educational and professional ambitions through their daughters, while others insisted on higher educational and technical skills as a 'fall-back' option in case of financial or marital difficulties. Technical skills and education are highly valued amongst the middle classes, leading to fierce competition for seats in engineering and medical colleges. With economic deregulation and liberalization, education is seen as the ticket to a good marriage both for women and men. The income that women bring into a family is very important to the family's security and its ability to anchor itself in the global economy and culture. However, education also fulfils another purpose – that of inculcating a rational, scientific temper, an understanding of current affairs and a broader worldview, all essential to living in the globalized market. Malini, who began our interview with the comment that getting a well-paid job is 'the reason

why I studied', mentioned a little later in her account that her education also fulfils a broader purpose:

> Now I feel what I studied has also made me a little broadminded
> and I'm aware. Suppose I go to a party or something, there's some
> subject they're talking about, I can also contribute because I have a
> little glimpse into what the world is. So I think now that studying
> has now taken a bigger picture than just getting marks and getting a
> job ... If a daughter-in-law is educated and has a job then even the
> in-laws give respect to her ideas. I have seen how people behave if
> they have one daughter-in-law who is working and one who is not
> working. They will give more weightage [to the one who is work-
> ing]. Even if I'm not working now my in-laws give me respect because
> I am educated. (Malini, 33, not currently in employment (resigned
> as manager), mother)

In Chapter 3 I argued that the nationalists promoted education of
women so that they might provide intelligent companionship to their
husbands and responsible mothering to their children (Chatterjee,
1989). This view continues to be a motivator in educating women. An
educated wife has the potential to augment the family income through
paid employment, to conduct herself more confidently within a globalizing culture, to provide emotional and practical support to her husband
and to take a proactive role in educating and mothering her children.
In addition a daughter's professional achievements add to the prestige
of her family and represent the 'respectable modernity' (Thapan, 2004)
to which the middle classes aspire. By supporting their daughters' and
daughters-in-law's professional success, middle class families display
their modernity to the wider kin-group and community. However, they
closely monitor women's pursuit of their ambitions and, when deemed
necessary, curtail them in the interests of family honour.

> I was never, never, never interested to go into engineering. I was
> interested in becoming a doctor from childhood and because my
> father wanted – he has given me that seed; he used to say me, 'See [be
> a] doctor, doctor, doctor' and I was really interested in science – very
> much. My marks were very good in science but in [the] entrance
> [examination] I could not get marks – may be three, four, marks were
> less and this community came into picture – where you have forward
> [upper castes] and backward community. For forward community
> limited seats were available[2] and moreover I wanted to continue with

my BSc in Speech and Hearing in Mysore but somehow I missed out because they [my parents] don't want to send me out from my native [town] and I was in my BSc Chemistry in my native [town] and then they told me engineering is there [available in her native town]. 'Okay, [I said] okay let me move onto that – my focus in engineering.' (Shreela, 29, manager, mother)

At first glance her status as an IT worker may indicate that Shreela is pursuing an individualist agenda for professional success, but on examination we see that this success is part of her duty to her family. Shreela's remarks suggest that the pressure to succeed drove her educational achievements; however, her parents' ambitions for her were influenced by the need to preserve their respectability by restricting her mobility. They refused to send her to another city to study. On her part Shreela reciprocated their investment in her education by taking the path they chose for her rather than the one she was interested in. While it could be argued that her parents' choice of engineering as a profession turned out in her favour, since it secured her a highly prestigious and remunerative IT career, it is also evident that her educational choices were family decisions rather than individualistic choices. Whilst aspirations to modernity and tradition are reconciled, this reconciliation restricts a woman's choices and constrains her individualism in contradiction with Giddens' (1991) arguments regarding the reflexive planning of one's life-course.

In contrast to the old middle class women, new middle class women such as Hema, Kanti and Christina did not enjoy high levels of support from their parents during their growing years. While new middle class parents recognize the importance of a college education, they are not aware of the nuances of the global labour market or how best to guide their children within it. In many cases the new middle class women interviewed were the first women in their families to have entered paid employment. If their mothers worked, they were usually in poorly paid, low-status jobs. Hema's parents wished to support her in taking an engineering degree but could not afford the fees, while Cristina's father could not afford to pay for further qualifications and also saw them as unnecessary.

When I was studying in college, I had to take up some [additional] early morning or evening classes, paying some thirty–forty thousand which was not affordable for me. My father could never understand why I should do these extra courses because he said, 'You are a graduate in computer science so you must be ahead of every-body.' ... He thought I would become a programmer. I knew it would never happen since I could not afford the extra courses. Everyone who was getting into software was either a BE [Bachelor of Engineering] or MCA [Master's in Computer Application]. We [who had a BSc in Computer Science] never had an opportunity. They used to just reject us on [our] face[s]. (Cristina, 29, administrator, mother)

May be I would have studied a little more, may be if I had to get an MBA – then my mom told me, 'I'll support you. Get an MBA [but I didn't].' Today my interests are HR [human resources]. So may be, you know – when I look at some managers here the calibre is very low. I can't expect somebody like that in an HR manager's position so I thought with my kind of outlook in life, with my kind of work experiences and the kind of recognition I've got in HR I could have done a better job. [If] I could have done something by now I would have been somebody. That support was not there for education – exposure nil! (Kanti, 35, administrator, mother)

Christina's limited means and her father's poor understanding of the job market restricted her opportunities. Similarly, Kanti implies, with bitterness, that her parents were unable to give her the advice required to make optimal use of the opportunities available because of globaliza-tion, even though her mother was willing to support her. Her accounts of her parents' financial insecurity, her father's absences and his alco-holism support her claim. Other new middle class women such as Hema and Nalini began work immediately after completing their schooling because of the financial situations of their families (their accounts are examined in greater detail in Chapter 7). However, both financed their own education, taking correspondence courses to gain additional quali-fications. The experience of these women indicates that in addition to parental support, cultural, social and economic capital play a crucial role in women's professional success.

Since I studied in Kannada medium till tenth and I had little difficul-ties in my career in expressing myself very clearly before others and communication difficulties. I never had it [wanted] for my son to face that so that could be the reason why I was speaking to him in English. Nowadays parents are well educated, their language is good. Where they do [since they speak English] in offices they do better in house to speak in English. (Nalini, 37, executive, mother)

Women from lower middle class backgrounds experience considerable difficulty in succeeding in the globalized labour market due to their lack of fluency in English. As Fernandes (2006) argues, English is not just a language or a skill but a marker of identity, and those who speak it fluently and without a trace of a regional accent have a distinct advantage in the globalized market – an advantage that Nalini does not enjoy. Hence she wishes her son to acquire it.

> I don't like hugging and kissing in front of anybody. Managers and bosses they are used to that kind of culture right? I was forced to do that. ... If these foreigners come in they don't shake hands. They will come and hug you, right? (The) first time they meet you – I mean that was little embarrassing for me. Now, I'm like, 'Yeah, since I'm working in (an) MNC, I need to adjust to this.' (Hema, 26, administrator, married)

In her research on urban Indian women in India, Tokita-Tanabe (2003) found that they make a crucial distinction between smartness and shyness – smartness being the ability to engage comfortably in the public sphere and interact freely but appropriately with men. Tokita-Tanabe's interviewees argued that unlike women from rural backgrounds they possessed the requisite degree of smartness; however, they also distanced themselves from other urban women whose behaviour suggested more permissive values. Hema's account indicates that she is learning this type of smartness even though it clashes with the values she was brought up to follow.

The women quoted above, Christina, Kanti, Hema and Nalini, all have undergraduate degrees. In addition, Nalini has taken several diplomas in personnel management and law, while Hema was taking an MBA course by correspondence at the time of the interview. Fernandes (2006) argues that due to restructuring and retrenchment many multinational companies are offloading complex managerial tasks to secretarial staff, requiring the latter to upgrade their skills but without structural mobility within the organizational hierarchy. In spite of their MBA degrees many secretarial and administrative staff find it difficult to join the management track due to their lack of cultural capital. They tend to remain in administrative jobs which are usually associated with short-term contracts and often at risk of retrenchment. In spite of their efforts to minimize this risk by increasing their qualifications, they have few options to enter the management track.

Their experience raises some questions about the implications of the reflexivity thesis that societies are moving towards a more rational, egalitarian and meritocratic order within late modernity. The findings of this research suggest along with previous work on the industry that privileges of class continue to influence individuals' life chances and that employees in the IT industry tend to be overwhelmingly from urban backgrounds (Upadhya, 2007; Upadhya and Vasavi, 2006; Krishna and Brihmadesam, 2006). A large proportion of Upadhya's (2007) interviewees identified as upper caste Hindu, indicating that caste and religion play a role in determining chances in the new transnational economy. Krishna and Brihmadesam (2006) find that many software professionals have two educated parents, suggesting that inherited social and economic capital is important to succeed in the global market. Contradicting not only the reflexivity thesis but also popular opinion regarding the meritocratic nature of the new economy, the collective findings of recent studies on the flagship industry of globalization, the IT industry, indicate that family background, medium of education (English versus regional language), and parents' occupational and class status can have considerable impact on an individual's professional success (or the lack of it).

Women of the lower castes and minority religions are usually doubly disadvantaged; therefore, the likelihood of finding women from these groups in the global economy is rare. In my own small sample, there were three women who identified as Christian and one who identified as Muslim by birth (married to a practising Hindu she follows both religions with no sense of conflict). Nearly all who mentioned caste identified as upper caste, but given the middle classes' reluctance to engage with what might be seen as a parochial identity, many did not directly mention their caste status, underscoring their regional or linguistic identities instead.

The smallness of sample does not allow for drawing generalizations regarding structural disadvantages created by religion and caste. However, I have attempted to analyse here the relative advantages and disadvantages created by class. My research indicates that women of the old middle classes such as Maya and Savita, and to a lesser extent Jaya and Shreela, not only had the advantage of parents who invested emotionally and financially in their education but also enjoyed certain subtler forms of cultural capital that are valued in the global market, including fluency in English, exposure to people outside of their home state and comfort in interacting with the opposite sex. As a consequence of cultural capital, old middle class women tend to enter the global labour market at the management-track level, while new middle class women tend to be more concentrated in administrative and support functions with limited growth opportunities. While some new middle class women such as Nalini and Hema invest in distance-learning programmes to augment their qualifications, they still find themselves lagging behind in the more subtle forms of cultural capital, such as the ability to socialize freely with male colleagues and the ability to speak English fluently.

I suggested in Chapter 2 that while Lash's notion of reflexivity's winners and losers is useful, it would be more useful to avoid seeing winning and losing as watertight compartments and to look for the gains and losses (limitations) that individuals and groups experience as a result of reflexivity. Old middle class women have certainly gained from the opportunities created by globalization, although the next chapter will argue that they continue to face disadvantages based on gender. On the other hand, new middle class women have gained some professional opportunities, but their capacity to maximize on these opportunities is limited by their class position. Moreover, globalization has created a number of jobs in areas such as customer care, administration and clerical work which are limited in terms of growth opportunities but give new middle class women access to unprecedented incomes and work experience in transnational companies. While they are aware of the limitations that they face, new middle class women are still grateful for the opportunities created by entering paid employment.

Motivations to work in the global economy

Social and emotional motivations

> Until I started working I was Ashok's daughter, Raghu's sister … People said, 'They're looking for [a suitable husband for] her', so I was always somebody's something. Now they're like [identifying my family as] Lathika's dad, Lathika's mother, Lathika's brother. They're all seeing me in new light; my parents are seeing me in new light … They're saying we never knew you were like this, we never knew. (Lathika, 33, manager, single)

> My mother-in-law used to expect a lot of things from me, like I should come early from work, take care of the child, like she is doing a favour for me and I have no responsibility. [But] I never thought [of giving up my job] because I knew that it would be a hell. At least eight hours I see the other world. In the house I have nobody except my child. [I] don't see or talk to anybody. (Cristina, 29, secretary, mother)

I got more confidence that any problem, anything, I can face it and I can resolve it. That confidence I didn't have earlier. May be after joining – [company name] I got more confidence, like it's a huge organization and you interact with more people. The managers are more supportive and they were pushing you to learn everything and they will make you to learn ... So that made me completely strong in whatever I am doing. Today you can check in – [company name] with anybody like any job that is given to Hema will be done. (Hema, 26, administrator, married)

It may be supposed that managerial jobs are associated with greater levels of autonomy, decision-making authority and opportunities for self-expression than administrative jobs which tend to be more routinized and controlled. However, irrespective of their position in the organizational hierarchy, women view paid work as a means of self-actualization and self-expression, of creating an identity independent from their families and contributing to the world (Dex, 2003; Irwin, 2005). Women's accounts indicate that paid work enhances their subjective sense of self, irrespective of class background and the nature of their jobs (Irwin, 2005). Even new middle class women whose poor access to cultural and educational capital limits their opportunities in the global economy find fulfilment in their professional lives. Does this mean that paid employment has enabled women to go through an 'individualization boost', as Beck and Beck-Gernsheim (2001: 55) suggest.

A closer examination of women's accounts indicates that the subjective motivations of self-fulfilment and self-expression are closely interwoven with social and financial motivations. A woman's sense of self-worth is closely interwoven with her family's pride in her achievements and their support for her career.

The way my parents look at me – I have a younger brother. It was assumed that he's going to have a career but for me it was a 'nice to have' thing but not some thing they thought I would pursue, you know. ... I think somewhere now they're proud of the fact that I have stuck it out. So if relatives or friends or whatever – I see them mentioning it more proudly. (Anita, 32, manager, mother)

Liddle and Joshi (1986) argued in the 1980s that by entering paid employment, women contribute not just to their family's income but also to its status; therefore, even when families are initially reluctant to promote a daughter's professional ambitions, they support them on seeing signs of success, such as a higher degree or prestigious job success-fully acquired. In contemporary globalized India having an employed daughter or a daughter-in-law is often a source of prestige for a family, and careers in IT are particularly aspirational in contemporary India since they are associated with high incomes, foreign travel, hi-tech work environments and a comfortable lifestyle. By promoting their daugh-ters' and daughters-in-law's careers in the global economy, families strengthen their positions within globalization and gain prestige and honour in the community. As in the case of the women interviewed by Liddle and Joshi, contemporary middle class women's seemingly indi-vidualistic achievement has an impact on the status of the entire family. As Shenoy's (2003) study of IT managers in India and the UK found, the pride that parents, husbands and children express of a woman's profes-sional achievements increases her sense of self-worth and, in the case of some participants, morally obliges her to succeed:

> The reason why I did, what I did and the kind of work I put in are largely because of the two of them – my mother and then my husband. The two of them are extremely ambitious for me more than I am, frankly, for myself. Because sometimes I wish I could take a little bit easy and do a little bit things on the side but they are like gunning at me. 'You're capable of it! You should do it. Why should you not do it? You've been educated for it. You should do it. You should make the best use of it.' So I have been pretty much focused on my career thereafter. (Maya, 37, manager, mother)

Paid employment also has a positive impact on the relationship between husband and wife, enabling them to share experiences and creating greater equality between spouses. Husbands are said to be more appreciative of the contributions and opinions of an employed wife. Cristina whose husband teaches human resources claims,

> He gives me good ideas, how to take the feedback from managers, how to respond to them. He says you should not escalate it immedi-ately, you should wait. ... I also tell him my experience. First he used to not be interested in what I am doing. Now he says he gets real examples for what he is teaching from [listening to my experiences] my work. (Cristina, 29, administrator, mother)

The sense of emotional well-being derived from self-expression, self-actualization and a life away from family also have an impact on women's family relationships and the quality of time she gives her children (Dex, 2003). Women who are in paid employment are conscious of the limited time they have with their children and attempt to maximize it by engaging in what they might consider high-value parenting tasks, reading with children, supervising homework, finding out about their day or cooking a favourite dish.

> Being at home from morning to night wasn't really giving me the satisfaction that 'Oh my kids are the best or I'm bringing them up in the best way', because I was not very happy. I'm happier when I'm at work and making a contribution to society and that whole thing of being independent and having a salary coming and the – just the whole feeling of doing something for myself that makes me happy. So if I'm happy then my family is happy. If I'm mentally more at peace with myself then my kids are happy, my husband is happy and everything and everyone around me is much more greener and better. (Geetika, 32, manager, mother)

The skills and experiences acquired in the workplace are transferable to home life: the skills of negotiating with and motivating junior employees are employed in parenting, time management at work helps women organize and manage the home efficiently and finally, exposure to contemporary issues, to the Internet and the communication skills acquired at work benefits children:

> For example when he had [to do an] environmental day project [for school] if I am at home [was a homemaker], I would have definitely have taken something from the newspaper, something from TV, I would have given him some experiences [examples/inputs]. But since I am working in HR, I am involved in all these activities. I know how we celebrate these things in the office. I could give him practical examples. It's a value addition to his education, no? (Nalini, 37, executive, mother)

> I think all the stress is worth putting up with and you know why? I feel happier about that tomorrow, I will be able to tell my daughter. I will be able to identify with what she goes through. I think things will be much easier then and I think things will be more structured, more supportive, many more women will be in the workplace. I didn't have anyone to turn to for advice and my mother didn't have the advice because she wasn't working in the first place. But I will

be able to handle her in a better manner, I will be a sounding board for these issues. I can at least hope to be a sounding board for – am I sounding very pompous [laughing]? (Anita, 32, manager, mother)

While Nalini draws on her experiences at work to educate her son, Anita derives satisfaction from the conviction that she is a role model to her daughter and will be able to support her in her own career; the daily challenge of managing multiple responsibilities becomes meaningful as she sees herself as an agent of change in her family and perhaps in the community as well. Women's satisfaction in their careers is not only subjective but also derives from how it enhances their relationships and the esteem it earns them in their families. They work not only for the sake of personal achievements but also to augment the status and prestige of their families. In the next section I argue that the same applies to the additional income that women's employment brings.

Financial motivations

Involvement in the global economy implies living within the individualistic ethos of global capitalism and consumerism. The availability of global brands, hire-purchase facilities, low-interest loans and salary advances have unleashed the consumerist appetites of the middle class (Gupta, 2000; Varma, 1998). The retail segment has increased phenomenally in the past decade, as seen from the growth of shopping malls and expansion of global brands in apparel, electronics and home appliances. While women use their incomes to buy lifestyle goods such as DVD players, hi-fi equipment, digital cameras and LCD televisions, these are not necessarily for personal use but for sharing within the family. Moreover, even though there is strong condemnation of the consumerist lifestyle of the middle classes from sections of the middle classes themselves, it is found that their attitude to money is fairly conservative (Upadhya and Vasavi, 2006). For instance two major arenas for investment of disposable income are real estate and education.

This is our own home. I mean this is our parents' place [where we currently live] so we don't shell out any money for rent or anything. A lot of it we invest. Traditionally it's been homes [which are the major area for investment] so we have a plot [of land] and we have a house. So that is what we've invested in. (Savita, 32, manager, mother)

We feel that we've made it on our own without any support from the family. We'd like to support our children for as long as we can, and whatever we are earning today is for them. For example may be my husband would have loved to study abroad but he couldn't because the income was – the capital wasn't there in the family to make him go there and study. So when we talk about our sons today we say we should have enough to give them that option, they should not grow up thinking that 'Oh, we want to go abroad and study but the money is not there.' (Geetika, 32, manager, mother)

It is apparent that real estate is an important investment option for the middle classes. Not only old middle class women but new middle class women also aspire to owning a home. Hema's first investment after marriage was in a one-bedroom flat, and Sumaiya on receiving my good wishes for her career at the end of our interview responded, 'And a flat, wish that I have my own house.' Across the middle classes women dedicate a large proportion of their income to their children's education. Continuing to uphold the value of education as their own parents did, they investigate options for their children that were not accessible to them: while new middle class women aspire to send their children to expensive private schools with English-language education, women from the old middle class look forward to sending their children abroad for further studies. Women's incomes thereby enable a family to stabilize its middle class status either in the present or in the near future and enable social upward mobility trough education and investments. However, while dual incomes enable middle class families to make additional investments, the capitalist free-market economy also has a dark side, as Anjana's remarks quoted earlier indicate, the risk of redundancy, fluctuations in financial markets and job insecurity. In such unpredictable circumstances women's incomes increase the family's security whilst enabling them to take advantage of the new economic opportunities.

Women's accounts suggest that their incomes tend to play one of two roles. The earnings of women such as Anita, Maya, Jaya and Geetika, who are married to men from the IT industry play an auxiliary role (though they are much valued) whereas the earnings of women whose husbands and fathers are not in the IT sector play a more pivotal role in the family income. This latter group includes Anjana, Swati, Hema, Sumaiya and Christina whose incomes are crucial to the family's middle class status. In other cases, both in the old and in the new middle classes, where husbands or fathers are not employed in the global economy, women's income is crucial to the family's position and security. The incomes of Anjana, Swati, Hema, Cristina and Sumaiya play this role. These women earn far more than their husbands and consequently undermine the latter's breadwinner status, even though they attempt to camouflage this in various ways. In both cases, most women tend to show ambivalence when discussing their financial contribution – theoretically they acknowledge its importance and feel a sense of satisfaction is supporting their parents, husband and children, but they also attempt to underplay its actual value if they feel that it threatens their husbands' prestige. Only a few new middle class women who find it impossible to deny the significance of their income to the family's financial situation openly acknowledge it.

> Basic needs he pays from his salary but all the luxuries, sudden emergency needs I take care [of]. That's why I'm managing [continuing in paid work] with all the problems [two young children and inadequate childcare]. (Cristina, 29, administrator, mother)

Cristina's income is essential to prevent her family from falling out of the middle class bracket. Her husband's lower paid job as a college lecturer earns them respectability, but her income provides the lifestyle that preserves that respectability and secures their middle class status. Comparing her account with Swati's, it is evident that women's incomes when they are higher than those of men could threaten the harmony of family life.

> With my husband from the day I got pregnant, he never used to get fruits, vegetables for me. A pregnant woman needs nutritious food so I used to buy fruits. Initially I discussed with my husband, should I give my salary to my mother-in-law and he said, 'I don't need it, you keep it', so whatever was required for me or for my house I used to buy it. I never used to look at my husband [to provide it]. I'm used to eating fruit but she used to never buy fruit and biscuits – like carrot is very important but she never used to buy that. She is a very miser[ly] person. She said [that] if I can't follow the rules in the house I can get out. ... I buy clothes for myself, my husband and child. I never had permission to replace anything old in the house, like music system or anything. She says what we have is enough. I don't have control over anything in the house. I go to the supermarket and pick up things [mainly food]. (Cristina, 29, administrator, mother)

If you see a public sector salary [Swati's husband works in the public sector] and an IT industry salary [her income] there is a huge scale [difference]. So I always keep this in mind that he should not feel inferior that she has money and she is spending. That is why she is taking all the decisions. It's more of giving him more importance. And I know he always respects my decision. It's not that he has to take decision and I don't have that confidence on my decision. It is more of giving him importance and more of giving him that belonging-ness. (Swati, 35, manager, mother)

Tactfully underplaying their financial independence enables women not only to avoid conflict but also but also to rely on their families to support them in care and domestic work, thereby creating the conditions for success within the individualistic values of the new economy. By consulting her husband before making major investments Swati attempts to show her respect for his position of authority. In contrast to Swati, Cristina not only finds it hard to mask her contribution to the family's finances, but her conflict-ridden relationship with her mother-in-law also makes her less motivated to do so. It may also be argued that her husband's refusal to take charge of her income, on the somewhat inaccurate premise that he does not need it, created conditions for her income to threaten existing authority structures in the family based on age and gender. Within new middle class families the earnings of a daughter-in-law can undermine the authority of her mother-in-law who might have waited years to reach her position of seniority.

Whatever might be the responses of individual families to their daughters' or daughters-in-laws' incomes, women's accounts almost universally indicate that they earn not to satisfy their own desires but to give their families a better lifestyle and a more secure future. Contrary to popular belief, earning an income does not make women independent of their families; rather their incomes are directly connected with their family responsibilities. Cristina spends the bulk of her income on necessities, such as supplementary food during her pregnancy; Geetika and Sumaiya save for their children's education; Nalini, Anjana and Jaya invest in real estate and Hema gives a portion of her earnings to her parents. While globalization has given middle class women access to unprecedented incomes, they do not use these incomes to create a life free from family ties and influences.

Conclusion

Middle class Indian women have more opportunities for education and employment than previous generations and more support from their families in accessing these opportunities. As Liddle and Joshi (1986) argue, families support women's employment because it augments their class status, enabling them to gain prestige within the caste and kin-group. It also helps the family realize the opportunities created by globalization and fulfil consumerist desires. For these reasons employment is no longer stigmatized as a sign of misfortune in the family; however, care is taken that women's employment does not threaten existing authority structures within families.

In the previous chapter I argued that while some of the more oppressive traditional discourses on women's positions within their families are losing ground, other discourses around the significance of marriage and motherhood remain resilient. This includes the discourse of individual choice and responsibility which often creates impossible standards for women in their roles as wives and mothers. This discourse is equally powerful in the labour market and the culture of transnational workplaces and serves to mask the structural inequalities that many women face.

Earlier feminist critiques of the late modernity thesis have argued that it tends to write out class and structural factors that influence individuals' capacity to create a reflexive biography (Skeggs, 2004; Mulinari and Sandel, 2009). Indian women's professional and educational choices are strongly influenced by their families' class position and the emotional and cultural capital that the latter can invest in them as well as their own efforts. These factors not only belie popular rhetoric about the meritocracy of the new economy, but they also raise questions about Giddens' assertion that people make individualized decisions about not only 'how to act but who to be' (1991: 81). While all women have access to opportunities created by globalization, their capacity to realize these opportunities depends on their position within the middle class and other structural factors.

Indian women's experiences within the new transnational economy suggest that Beck and Beck-Gernsheim's (2001) thesis might have overlooked the relationship between the labour market and family life. While the labour market (particularly in the private sector) in India is indeed becoming more individualized, women's accounts of their motivations to remain in paid employment indicate a strong need to contribute to their families and strengthen their position within a globalized economy. Indian women attempt to conform to the individualistic values of the labour market in order to support their families. In the next chapter I investigate how families support women in performing their professional roles by sharing care work and the repercussions this support has for women.

6
Managing Paid Employment and Family Life

My husband has always supported me. He never said, 'Quit your job.' At the same time he also never made it his problem. It was always my problem to figure out how to do things. 'You want to work, that's fine. Figure it out, who's going to look after the kids.' Even now everything and anything to do with the house is my problem, not his – it's just the way things have been. I may complain, not to him, but to others about it, or crib to myself but at the end of the day there's peace in the house. For me that's very important. (Geetika, 32, manager, mother)

Beck and Beck-Gernsheim (2001) argue that the labour market and family are often in conflict within late modernity because the needs of the labour market, flexibility, individualization and mobility, are antithetical to the needs of family life, stability, rootedness and altruism. Since individualism enjoys high purchase in late modernity, workers are expected to create a highly individualized career path, to be agile, adaptable and mobile. They contend that individualization puts high stress on the family as two individuals struggle to reconcile their divergent career paths, both unwilling to sacrifice their professional aspirations for the benefit of the relationship. This leads to what they call 'a long and bitter battle' between the sexes (Beck and Beck-Gernsheim, 1995: 14). Women are believed to be particularly vulnerable in this conflict because they are caught between the traditional expectation of living for others and the late modern ideal of living a life of one's own. While Beck and Beck-Gernsheim's point of reference is the neoliberal society of contemporary Western Europe, their arguments imply a certain universality in these social trends.

Geetika's remarks above suggest that when home and workplace are in conflict, it is women who manage the situation. Most old middle class women view their presence in the workplace as a privilege rather than a right, while new middle class women tend to view it as a necessity. While they realize the unfairness of the dual burden of paid and unpaid work, they prefer to manage their feelings (and those of others) rather than confronting the skewed division of labour in the home. In this chapter I examine the consequences of this dual burden for women and their strategies for managing it. Since mothers experience much bigger challenges in balancing the demands of the two spheres, I concentrate on their experiences in the bulk of the chapter. This is not to deny that single women and married women without children (or even men) face work-life-balance challenges, but the crucial years in early stages of women's careers which demand high commitment and long hours coincide with marriage and the birth of children. Marriage and motherhood are important rites of passage for women in several cultures and demand that women rework their priorities in a way that men are rarely expected to. However, the priority given to the identities of wife and mother in India makes this period particularly demanding for Indian women (Parthasarthy, 1994; Shenoy, 2003).

As in the previous chapter, I suggest that one might cautiously generalize from the experiences of middle class women in the IT industry to middle class women working in the private sector in general. The IT industry is seen as a trendsetter for progressive human resource policies. Its policies related to women employees have been adopted by other manufacturing and service industries such as biotechnology and banking. Consequently women's experiences of managing paid work and family life in these industries are likely to mirror the experiences of women in the IT.

It may be said that the IT industry is responsible for popularizing the concepts of 'work-life balance' and 'diversity management' in India. However, it is important to note differences in how diversity management is understood in the Indian and Euro-American contexts. While diversity management in European or North American context might suggest the existence of a variety of categories of difference along the axes of race, ethnicity, age and gender, in Indian industry diversity management is usually associated with gender diversity. It is not in the interests of the IT industry to associate itself with the sensitivities of caste, religion, ethnicity and other forms of social and cultural diversity in India. Addressing such questions might lay it open to equal opportunity lawsuits and public enquiries into the exact numbers it employs from minorities and marginalized communities. Therefore it is safer for the industry to equate diversity management with creating opportunities for women. The question arises as to what happens when the industry speaks of (gender) diversity management, suggesting that diversity is an asset to be harnessed for productivity and profit.

It has been suggested that the institutionalization feminism can dilute its political agenda, or worse, subvert its emancipatory potential. Elizabeth Prügl (2011) in her examination of discourses of diversity management argues that they produce both empowerment and constraint, enabling women's concerns and experiences to enter policy making but also making feminist knowledge into a means of 'governing' gender relations and conduct, in the Foucauldian sense. In the Indian IT industry the language of women's empowerment exists alongside a long-hours culture premised on a traditional gendered division of labour at home. In examining women's challenges in managing paid work and care, this chapter will broadly address questions of what happens when neoliberal notions of choice and feminist ideas of empowerment co-exist within organizational discourse.

The IT industry's pro-women image is celebrated in the press through articles with titles such as 'Women on Top!' (Alexander, 2007), 'IT's a Woman's World' (Ramalingam, 2007), 'India's New Worldly Women' (*Business Week*, 2005) and 'The Changing Indian Woman' (Bhagat, 2007). It often reiterates its commitment to increasing the number of women in its workforce (claimed to be over 30% (Alexander, 2007)) and to supporting their progress through a number of policy initiatives (Alexander, 2007; Nayare Ali, 2006; Ramalingam, 2007) which could include recruitment targets, the option of extending the mandatory three-month maternity leave, company transport for those working late, a crèche for children and support for home-based work (telecommuting) by providing employees above a certain pay grade with Internet connectivity at home. It is claimed that women are allowed to select assignments that are less demanding whilst their children are young. While a few articles do examine the conflicts between professional and family priorities (Dyuti, 1998; Padmanabhan, 2008), the discourse in the press is highly celebratory.

Upadhya and Vasavi (2006) argue that although the IT industry claims to have a high proportion of women (about 30–35%), many of them are concentrated in low-profile work. Women engineers are in roles such as programming and testing rather than the more prestigious roles of architecture and project management. Women are also over-represented in support functions such as human resources and administration.

They attribute women's under-representation in the industry and their concentration in low-profile work to three factors, women's inability to work late due to issues of safety and domestic responsibilities, their exclusion from informal networks and the lower number of hours they work in comparison with men. While the first two of these findings are corroborated by my research, I argue later in this chapter that women might not be able to work in the office late at night but work the same number of hours as men (or more) from their homes.

While the IT industry claims to support a flexible working culture wherein employees can choose their work hours and work remotely from home (teleworking), the actual implementation of work-life-balance policies may not mirror the industry rhetoric. Both my research and that of Upadhya and Vasavi found that women who choose flexitime after childbirth may find themselves sidelined when it comes to promotions and that individual managers may block the implementation of flexitime in their teams due to the pressures of work and the discontent it creates amongst (male) team members who do not use flexitime. The industry's party-line is that employees are given choices and that they are responsible for the consequences of those choices on their careers.

> Whoever said this is a level-playing field? Whoever said that everyone starts at the starting line and everyone runs the same race? That's not true. It is not a level-playing field. It's true [that] some people have advantages [and] some people don't. And you live with work with whatever it is that you have. It's not that I am less sympathetic with people who have these issues. My issue is after asking for all these, all the additional support that you need at the workplace, you can't also expect to be paid the same, to have the same career progression at the same pace as somebody else who didn't ask for those and is still working. That is unfair to the rest of the workforce. (Maya, 37, manager, mother)

A mother of a two-year-old child, Maya, has worked hard to reach her current position as the director of human resources at her company. She argues that she has not asked for support or 'concessions' at the workplace to enable her to reach this position (in the next chapter where I discuss her account in greater detail it will become evident that she can avoid asking for support at work partly because of her parents' support at home). From her comments above she seems to be aware that the workplace is not a 'level-playing field' since not everyone has 'support systems' (parents or in-laws who can take over childcare) but also does not see it as an organizational responsibility to create one. Her comments suggest that in spite of the rhetoric of work-life balance, the logic of the neoliberal market governs the organization and its human resource policies. The valourization of choice and responsibility points to what Mathew Adams (2006) calls the darker side of reflexivity wherein choices are ostensibly offered to everyone, yet some individuals are in a better position than others to make the most of these choices based on class, gender, race or ethnicity. Supporters of the neoliberal logic often fail to account for this difference in access to choice.

Organization of work in the globalized workplace

> They're here to save costs, so the bottomline is 'get your work done at low costs'. (Anita, 32, manager, mother)

The Indian IT industry grew in the 1990s on its ability to provide skilled labour at lower costs to the advanced economies of Europe and America. In their ethnography of the industry Upadhya and Vasavi (2006: 8) suggest that the 'outsourcing of software development projects by American companies to Indian services providers, the setting up of offshore development centres by multinationals in India and the burgeoning of international call centres and other such back office operations' resulted in the phenomenal growth of the IT industry in the past two decades.

The industry strongly values flexibility, individualization and customer satisfaction (Upadhya and Vasavi, 2006). Most roles require some mobility though engineers and managers are usually expected to be most mobile, travelling according to clients' needs and taking up overseas assignments as required. Those who remain in India engage in 'virtual migration' (Aneesh, 2006); that is, they are available online to clients irrespective of time differences. Given the logic of minimizing outlay, organizations are fairly lean and often go through restructuring (downsizing) to cut down jobs.

As I argued in the previous chapter flexibility also has another facet: many employees are hired on temporary contracts which can be terminated if market conditions change. Individual employees are expected to take responsibility for their own career progression, training and professional success rather than depending on companies to take care of them till they retire. A highly individualized, non-unionized workforce cannot work collectively to change industry policies or work conditions. Thus the offer of flexibility is not always beneficial to the employee.

The values of flexibility and mobility are closely associated with what has in previous literature been identified as 'ideal worker norms' (Wajcman, 1998; Hochschild, 1997; Williams, 2000; Pocock, 2003). The ideal worker is someone who does not have personal responsibilities and is single-mindedly devoted to the workplace. Such employees have no family obligations to distract them from work and are 'available to take on extra assignments, respond to emergency calls, or relocate any time' (Hochschild, 1997: xix). This description, as Arlie Hochschild (1997) argues, rarely fits anyone, except possibly the very young: most workers have children, partners, elderly parents and homes which demand attention. In the post-industrial period where both partners are in paid work, neither can take complete responsibility for care work in the home; however, ideal worker norms remain the yardstick by which workers are evaluated. Even when non-traditional ways of working are available (part-time work, telecommuting or job sharing), the most powerful, prestigious and highly remunerated jobs tend to be those most closely associated with ideal worker norms (Williams, 2000). In women's accounts of working in the Indian IT industry, this association of success with total commitment to work and de-prioritization of family life is evident.

> Indians by nature are very workaholic in temperament. You can't seem to draw the line between your work and your family life. The concept of work-life balance does not exist. It has just started creeping into the minds of some people. Nobody will go home at six o'clock. They will waste their time in meetings and stuff like that, but they will not manage their time so that they can go home at six o'clock. The general culture is that you have to work long and hard to be successful in this industry. (Rupa, 28, manager, married)

The IT industry favours a long-hours culture wherein employees are expected to work well beyond the global standard of a 40-hour week. They are expected to be available on the telephone or online on weekends and on holidays. The need to deliver services within competitive timeframes and save costs leads to tight deadlines and high levels of work intensification. For instance, Savita, whose previous assignment was to head a team responsible for maintaining products for overseas clients, was often required to respond to clients' queries late in the night via conference calls involving several people across multiple locations.

> Until a year back I used to be on call so I would come home and I would have to get on a con-call [conference call] because something

somewhere in some part of the world had gone wrong. So I would have to be available for thirteen, fourteen, sixteen hours a day. (Savita, 32, manager, mother)

I leave home by eight thirty, otherwise by nine. It takes about an hour and work starts here and till I come to a logical break I don't go. I should feel like most of the items I have scheduled for the day is done and I'm at a logical point to leave. So many times I leave at around – any time after seven thirty, usually seven thirty, eight and at times it becomes [late]. (Jaya, 33, manager, mother)

While late-night work is usually associated with software maintenance projects, managers in other functions also report working from home early in the morning, late in the evening or on weekends. They share instances of taking work-related calls while on holiday, whilst taking care of sick children and during family celebrations and religious festivals. Managers are expected to participate in training events on weekends and organize after-work parties to boost team morale and introduce subordinates to clients.

Managers such as Savita and Jaya are accountable for generating revenues; consequently they feel pressured to show high levels of commitment to work. It has been suggested that working long hours can be 'identity affirming' (Lewis, 2003: 349) in those occupations where a culture of intensive work and client-centredness prevails. Jaya's remarks about her workday suggest that some of the pressure to work long hours is internal rather than organizational. For managers who have a relative degree of autonomy and opportunities for self-expression in their role, enjoyment of work might result in long hours. However, as Lewis argues, the 'choice' to work long hours may be influenced by factors such as peer pressure or company. In the case of one manager, the pressure to switch back from flexible to regular hours came from a subordinate:

If you are a lady boss then you are a very easy target. 'She doesn't stay late. She doesn't travel. How are we to deliver? She can't blame it all on us.' (Anita, 32, manager, mother)

While managers' enjoyment of their work might mitigate the frustration generated by the long-hours culture of the industry, administrators and executive assistants feel forced to work long hours because of the work schedules of their managers. Kanti's, Hema's and Cristina's workdays depend on their manager's schedules and ways of working. While Hema's manager is fairly sensitive to her family commitments, Kanti's and Cristina's managers tend to be more demanding. Cristina complains that her workday is highly unpredictable due to the haphazard working methods of her manager. She resents his expectation that she should be available beyond office hours (including giving him a wake-up call if he has an early morning meeting) but feels unable to complain.

> I prefer to go back at six but normally it gets late. They [managers] don't realize that it's time to leave. I have to help him to claim his telephone bills. I can't do it alone. I need to sit with him to identify his personal calls. He wants me to book vehicles for his relatives who come to visit Bangalore. Even on Christmas Day, he called me ten times. He didn't wish me for Christmas. He didn't even ask me whether he can disturb me. Men can say 'no' but I am not very assertive. (Christina, 29, administrator, mother)

Given that the city's infrastructure has not caught up with its growth, traffic jams are a common feature of daily life and public transport is uncertain. This tends to make the workday even longer and somewhat unpredictable. While some women in managerial positions travel by car, others use company transport (air-conditioned buses) and a few use public transport (usually auto-rickshaws). Amongst women who are in administrative/executive positions, Hema has a car while Kanti, Cristina and Nalini use a combination of different types of transport to reach the office: either they are dropped by their husbands (on scooters or in cars) to a bus stop or auto stand or they take a ride part of the way with other female colleagues. The opening of the metro rail in the city is intended to reduce commuting problems, but it will take some years to become fully operational. While the beginning of the workday is dictated by children's school timings or essential meetings, the end of the workday depends on the volume and urgency of work, the timings of company transport and the availability of auto-rickshaws, factors which add to what Hochschild calls the 'time famine' that participants experience (1997: 199).

> The whole day goes in that struggling so that you don't have to spend that extra one and half hours. My coffee times are restricted, my tea times are restricted because I know if I waste that extra fifteen minutes something else is going to pile up. (Swarna, 31, manager, mother)

Psychological and personal costs of the long-hours culture

The demands of a hectic work schedule on the one hand and the unequal gendered division of labour in the home on the other hand result in the time famine that women experience. In the industrial period there was a clear dichotomy between home and work. The home was constructed as an idyllic space where individuals might escape from the pressures and anxieties of the world, and women were charged with nurturing and protecting this space. In the post-industrial period where both men and women are working and where the telephone, email and other forms of communication bring paid work into the home, these boundaries cannot be stringently maintained. Yet women continue to feel a sense of responsibility to protect the home from the demands of the workplace. They often lose the battle to do so, given their own presence in the workplace and their limited capacity to negotiate their conditions of work. The failure to protect their home-lives from the intrusion of work can add to their sense of frustration.

> I guess my life is so fine-tuned to the last second that even if there is a little bit of delay I get very agitated. So I guess I'm a little impatient, that's the issue ... It could be that I get done with this, I need to get into something else and when that gets done then I get to go somewhere else and if any one of these things in the chain gets – and it always does, right, you can't help it – especially with the boy [her son], it always does. He's supposed to wake up at nine in the morning but he decides to sleep in further and he refuses to wake up or we want him to wear his sweater and he's jumping round the house and he thinks it's a game and we're progressively getting delayed in the day. ... I get very short-tempered which is not very good because I was never a short-tempered person. (Maya, 37, manager, mother)

Given the division of labour between the male breadwinner and female carer in the industrialized period, the schedules of the home followed that of the workplace but could be run in a more relaxed manner. In the post-industrial period both partners are in the workplace, resulting in the stress of coordinating two (competitive) work schedules in addition to schedules of children; the home has become constraining and stressful for adults and children (Runté and Mills, 2004). The need for speed, efficiency and coordination makes it as Taylorized[1] and regulated as the workplace (Hochschild, 1997; Runté and Mills, 2004). As work enters the home, it becomes as much a site of stress and competition as the workplace.

> I got a good job. It was again a telecom company here and it was again a good job. I had a really challenging role. I was for two years there, more than two years, two and a half but since it was a telecom company it was really difficult. If you have seen a telecom company: you come home and you get a call immediately. It was that type of support which was expected. I used to talk for one hour, two hours on the phone [after returning from work], I used to get some migraine headaches. (Shreela, 29, manager, mother)

The 'time famine' (Hochschild, 1997: 199) that participants experience has serious consequences for their health and emotional well-being. In the previous section Maya described how she has developed a tendency to lose her temper due to her hectic schedule. Stress is also expressed in acute physical symptoms that participants report: back-aches, high or low blood pressure, sleeplessness, spondylosis, migraines, recurrent colds, respiratory illnesses and a sense of exhaustion. Savita shared how her postpartum depression extended much longer because of the demands of her job. The mothers I interviewed shared the psychological cost of anxiety and guilt that is felt by mothers across the world (Pocock, 2003; Posner, 1992; Brannen and Moss, 1991). They claim that they crave for sleep, silence and the luxury of doing nothing (see also Hochschild, 1989, on the craving for sleep).

> One of the things I noticed is wherever, I am whatever I am doing, I'm always thinking I'm so pre-occupied, office, home, office, home, office, home. The wheels are churning constantly and I think that sort of makes you very tired at times. So when I took a week off during the Diwali break, everybody's like, 'You didn't go on a holiday?' And I was like, 'No, I just wanted to be alone. I just wanted to do my stuff and eh – so that's it.' (Savita, 32, manager, mother)

When confronted with the image of a 'proper mother' who is always available to her children and does not need to juggle the demands of employment and motherhood, women feel judged not only by their own families but also by colleagues, neighbours and the wider community. Pressured by popular discourses on intensive mothering and child development, women tend to feel responsible for any perceived 'failure' in their children's academic success or social and emotional adjustment (Hattery, 2001). Pocock's (2003) description of 'mother-wars' – criticism women who work face from those who stay at home with their children – is echoed in Anita's account. Her neighbour's repeated assertion that by staying at home she would really 'see her daughters blossom' brings on fresh waves of guilt for a mother who is already torn between work and home.

> I was driving home in the rain trying to navigate my way ... and then I had my neighbour calling up, saying that your daughter is standing outside [the house] crying and that is really the pits. You really feel like a heel. I like, appreciate the good intentions of the neighbour but the next day she told me, 'Anita, don't you think you should quit? It's not fair on the kid [to be taken care of by maids].' And this neighbour of mine has left her career completely – her nature as a woman, you know – she's had her child. When I got home things were very much under control. You know how children are, you know a four-and-half, five-year-old. She must have been throwing a tantrum but I trust the maid – she's an affectionate lady. (Anita, 32, manager, mother)

If Anita felt judged by her neighbour, then the judgement that Swati experienced came from much closer home:

> For one day this year, my daughter's birthday, there were some urgent meetings. I had come to office and I left at twelve thirty. Then at two thirty my manager called me, 'Can you please come to ——— [name of client company] at three thirty, we have a really urgent meeting.' I went there and my daughter was crying and my in-laws were very unhappy with it. 'Just one day you have taken leave, you went to office and again your manager is calling you.' So I went to ——— [name of client company]. The meeting was not that urgent. There is no point in calling somebody from daughter's birthday. When he called me [I told him] her friends will come by four thirty. 'No, no by then you'll come back.' It's not that I will come back. I have to do the arrangements and at the same time her dad is not there [living in Bangalore], so if she feels that something is not happening she calls him up and says, 'Daddy you are not here. Mamma did not do this, she did not do that.' So he says, 'Whatever you do for yourself [is fine] but you need to take care of the kid. You also need to give her time.' (Swati, 35, manager, mother)

Swati not only felt torn between her manager's claims on her time and those of her daughter, she also faced criticism from her husband for failing in her duty as a mother. Her daughter's complaints seem to have heightened her sense of frustration. When juggling the needs of their families and demands of the workplace, women speak of their dilemmas as choices between various injustices: 'injustice to my children', 'injustice to my mother/mother-in-law (who provides substitute care)', 'injustice to myself, after all I've worked hard to develop my skills', 'injustice to my parents who invested in my education'. In the previous chapter I discussed how important Swati's income is to her family, but her husband seems to have overlooked that when describing her work as something that she 'does for herself'.

For women whose families are not completely dependent on their income (or if families underplay the importance of women's incomes), the psychological costs of the long-hours culture are evident in the endless soul searching or guilty comparisons to their mothers, mothers-in-law and friends who are totally immersed in the home. Women tend to be self-critical for having made a choice in favour of their own need for self-actualization and therefore carry a burden of guilt for 'stealing' time from children to and giving it to the workplace. However, even those whose families need their income suffer guilt and anxiety on leaving their children to go to work. Cristina and Kanti, who are forced to leave their children with rather uncooperative in-laws, speak of their anxiety that the children are being neglected at home. As administrative staff they cannot easily negotiate for flexible work timings. When asked if she would like to continue in paid employment, Kanti replied with tears in her eyes:

> If I didn't have to earn money and pay my loans I'd just sit [at home], take care of my kid, cook well ... I never gave [her] anything from day one. Till today I never gave [her] anything. I don't cook anything for her, neither does she ask me because she knows that I don't have time. (Kanti, 34, administrator, mother)

Kanti's reply raises questions about the industry's commitment to gender equality. It raises the question whether a capitalist enterprise located within the logic of transnational markets can ultimately promote the rights of its female workforce in a meaningful way. Anita's remark in the previous section draws attention to the Indian IT industry's position as a service provider to Europe, America and East Asia. In its commitment to saving costs and maximizing profit by increasing the speed and efficiency of projects, the industry ultimately cannot provide meaningful work-life-balance solutions to the most vulnerable sections of its workforce.

Organizational strategies for work-life balance: The 'flexibility and choice' rhetoric

Unlike many European countries where the state provides care for young children, enabling parents to stay at home while children are young, in India employees are expected to make their own care arrangements. It may be argued that in India the state has other priorities with regard to the majority of Indian women who are not in the privileged position of the middle classes, including their mortality, safety, health and employment opportunities. The responsibility of providing solutions for childcare falls on organizations. However, the cultural tendency to provide care within families has historically enabled employers to abdicate the responsibility of providing childcare while giving lip service to the issue. Earlier research on employed women indicates that substitute care is inevitably sought within extended families (Liddle and Joshi, 1986). Therefore the IT industry's self-proclaimed commitment to work-life balance and flexible working arrangements has received great appreciation in popular media.

IT companies claim to offer work-life-balance options such as flexitime and teleworking (see Rathore and Sachitanand, 2007), leaving employees to construct their own work day. In reality though, these options are usually offered only to those on the management track and at the discretion of the individual's line manager. Some female managers such as Jaya, Anita and Savita have taken the extended maternity leave (on partial pay) option after childbirth, but the administrative staff could not afford to do so. Amongst the twenty-six women interviewed, ten had been able to negotiate for flexible work options with their managers. In all cases they opted to work from home whenever required. In some cases this option was exercised by leaving late for the office or returning home early to spend the rest of the workday teleworking via the phone and the Internet. For others there were specific days of the week when they worked from home. Of the ten, all were married, seven were mothers and all but one was in the management track. There was no difference between managers' access to flexibility based on their role or function. The only administrator who used the teleworking option, Hema, did so only in emergencies, for example, if a family member was unwell. Kanti, another administrator in the same company, could not take the flexitime option due to the chaotic nature of her home life and her conflict-ridden relationship with her husband and in-laws, which makes it difficult for her to ask for their support in childcare:

> My daughter is so boisterous; three o'clock she's back. Where's the time for me to sit down at my computer and do all my work when she's not going to let me do anything at all? And I can't log in late in the night. I need to sleep, she needs to sleep, otherwise we won't get up in time to go to school – lots of things are involved. (Kanti, aged 35)

The option of teleworking presumes that employees will have the privacy, space and quiet time to work at home. This is often not the case within many new middle class homes. Women from new middle class families who usually form the non-managerial cadre in the IT industry might not have access to a quiet space or enough domestic help to take care of children while they continue with paid work in the home. However, given their limited means to hire full-time nannies and maids, they are the ones who are most in need of support with their caring responsibilities. The discourse of flexibility does not account for these differences in their needs and home situations. Moreover they tend to find less sympathy for their professional commitments in their families, as the accounts of women discussed in Chapter 5 suggest. In this construction of the reflexive choice-making individual, Giddens doesn't account for these differences in individuals' access to choice.

Workers who choose flexible working practices face another barrier in the home, which is that family members may resent their continued disengagement in family life even when they are physically present at home. Once they return from work women are expected to resume those responsibilities that their mothers or mothers-in-law have been taking on in their absence.

> Some people feel that working from home is very good but working from home is actually horrible. It's like all the times your phone will be ringing, everyone will be ringing. Now-a-days after having this mobile and everyone having this mobile number is horrible. ... Working from home is all that time you are doing the office work, getting calls and whoever is at home, he or she will feel that you will do something for that person. All the time [I am] talking on the phone. Sometimes my daughter also gets irritated. 'Mamma why are you at home? You go to office!' My maid also says, 'Didi [older sister] you better go ...' (Swati, 35, manager, mother)

In spite of these barriers many managers do take up the option if the only alternative is to give up paid employment. However, the unspoken criticism of colleagues, demands of clients and expectations of managers might pressure women to work twelve to sixteen hours a day, especially in software jobs. Therefore when women choose flexible working options they attempt to prove their professionalism by working harder than others (see also Hochschild, 1997, on peer pressure):

> I left that company to join a smaller set-up, just to ensure that I have more quality time with my family and my child. And the first condition that I put to them ... I told them I'm going to be available for them at a time when it is more suited to my family life. I don't shy away from working late or something but I will work remotely at home, but I will not stretch my day in the office. I have to physically be there for my child. That was a compromise I had to do with my profession. (Anjana, aged 33)

> Well, you know the way guys work. [They come in at] any time between eight thirty or nine thirty and they stay till about ten [in the night]. And it's like a straight twelve hours or whatever and they take about seven, eight smoke breaks which is about twenty minutes each and eh whereas so that's about two, three hours. I don't smoke, I don't take as many breaks. I get in, I have work and till I get out I'm at my table. I hardly have time to get out on the terrace [for a cigarette] and all that stuff which they don't realize. Plus I work from home two or three hours in a day [in the], mornings and nights. Put together, typically my work hours are about eleven hours of office work and four hours of travel on the road. (Savita, 32, manager, mother)

Women who do take flexitime may end up working longer than employees who are at the office in order to show their commitment, but without the benefit of 'face time' (visibility in the office) that would position them as serious workers with high career aspirations. Their work is invisiblized in the same manner that housework is invisiblized by its performance within the private domain of the home. Women on flexitime also lose out on opportunities to network informally both during and after office hours which is essential to career growth (Shenoy, 2003; Posner, 1992).

Having ostensibly provided options for creating a flexible work schedule, the industry adopts the neoliberal stance that creating a work-life balance is the responsibility of the employee. Maya, the senior human resource manager mentioned earlier, argues that it is up to each employee to articulate their value to the organization and that managers always support employees who are valued. Such a discourse fails to challenge cultural assumptions about the primacy given to work and does not hold the employer accountable for employee well-being. Susan Lewis, Richenda Gambles and Rhoana Rapoport (2007) argue that the discourse of work-life balance overlaps with the neoliberal discourse of choice, but these two discourses overlook the gendered contexts and long-hours culture in which choices exist. In the case of Indian women it may be argued that class and geography also influence choices. Given the industry's position as a provider of cheap labour to European and American markets, Indian women's choices are constrained by the need for speed and productivity.

Developing further on the theme of discourses, Steve Fleetwood (2007) argues that flexibility can either be employee friendly or employer friendly. The discourse of employee friendliness masks the ways in which flexible working practices may benefit the employer at the expense of the employee. In Anjana's and Savita's cases, for instance, their commitment to their work is undeniably beneficial to their employers; however, the invisiblization of the work they do from home could compromise their career growth as Anjana suggests.

Individual strategies for managing paid work and care

Combining paid and unpaid care work by invoking reciprocal obligations

The dual burden of care work and paid work has been well documented across cultures (Dex, 2003; Wajcman, 1998; Hochschild, 1989; Pocock, 2003; Shenoy, 2003). Amongst my participants the 'second shift' of care work (Hochschild, 1989) includes cooking, cleaning, shopping for the family and supervising domestic help. All the participants in the research reported having some form of paid domestic help except Hema and Sumaiya who prefer to do housework themselves. Both have fairly small homes and supportive husbands but spend at least a couple of hours every day on housework. In addition Sumaiya also cares for her two-year-old child. Women in administrative positions can only afford part-time maids, while most women in managerial positions can afford servants, cooks and live-in maids who take on the more onerous household tasks (Liddle and Joshi, 1989; Crompton, 2006). However as Geetika put it when she interrupted the interview (at her office) to take a call from the maid, women often 'run the home on remote control' via the telephone, giving instructions on cooking and housekeeping and checking if children have eaten, washed and completed their homework. They also get calls from the childminder and the child (with questions, complaints and updates), which they try to take as discretely as possible since their supervision of domestic work from the office is often criticized and ridiculed by male colleagues.

Given the availability of cheap domestic labour in India, Indian women's second shift is not as onerous as that of women in other cultures; however, given that housework is rarely shared equally with men, they still take a large share of both the actual work and the planning and organizing of it. They also take on a burden of guilt that they are not performing it according to prevalent cultural standards. Women rarely oppose this unfair division of labour, as I suggested in the introduction of this chapter. In their accounts they appreciate the contribution of their husbands however small it might be, comparing them to those of other men: 'our husbands are better than our fathers and our sons will be better than our husbands' (Anjana, 33, manager). As Hochschild (1989) argues, the intimacy of the marital tie requires some concealment of the inequalities in it.

While housework can be offloaded onto the market, the care of children needs to be managed much more carefully. It has been argued that since care is conceptualized as an altruistic and emotionally charged activity, marketized care is seen as inferior to unpaid care (Folbre and Nelson, 2000). Sending the child to a crèche carries the stigma associated with marketized care; it connotes less control for mothers and more possibility of neglect since the child-to-adult ratio is greater than at home. Women use it sparingly, only in cases where there are no alternatives.

Hiring a nanny or childminder is considered the next best option since they provide care within the home and can be managed more closely. But they are not considered reliable as they are prone to absenteeism. They might not take the same pains as parents or grandparents take to coax a fussy child to eat, ensure that the child does her homework or washes well. They might allow more television viewing than the mother considers optimal or compromise the child's safety by carelessness or oversight. A responsible maid who is patient with the child and follows instructions carefully is invaluable. Women therefore take pains to keep such maids satisfied, offering food, clothes and loans of money as incentives.

I look after my maids very well, I have always been treating them like family members. ... I've kept my kitchen open for the servants.

> I think food is a very important thing for them. ... The girl who looks after my children, she needs to be well fed and well looked after so that she looks after my children. ... That's the arrangement I have kept from the beginning as far as domestic help is concerned. (Geetika, 32, manager, mother)

The best form of substitute care is therefore that of grandparents who are believed to be motivated by love for the grandchild. While this reduces anxieties regarding the child's well-being, some women are concerned about not having complete control over their children's upbringing, burdening their parents in their old age and 'giving up' their responsibilities. To reduce the burden on the grandparents, women employ maids to take on the more onerous tasks of caring for children under the supervision of the grandparents. However, by calling on their assistance, women become closely implicated in reciprocal care exchange with the elders. For this strategy to work, parents or in-laws need to live close by or within the same household. If this is not possible, older children might be sent on extended visits to grandparents during school holidays. However, one participant, Shreela, decided to send her one-year-old to live for nearly a year with her parents as they could not move to Bangalore. Although ambivalent about her decision, she attempts to justify it:

> Back in January, I felt it's high time I got to my normal routine and it was really a tough decision that I made to leave my son there but I didn't have an option. Day cares in Bangalore start only from [when the child is] two years basically – [my husband and I decided to] let him also explore things from his side which might be good for his future also. [She indicated later in the interview that she wanted her child to be more independent and a 'risk taker'.] Moreover, my brother's daughter is there for company so I think he is having good time and we are also travelling [to see him] every alternate weekend. (Shreela, 29, manager, mother)

Servicing the care debt

By invoking reciprocal kinship obligations as substitute care for their children, women incur a 'care debt' which is reciprocated in two ways: through tangible efforts and through symbolic gestures. Tangible efforts may include preparation of meals, including the older generation in leisure pursuits or planning leisure activities around their interests, spending time together discussing the day, driving them to visit friends and relatives or escorting them to the doctor, to family celebrations such as weddings, poojas (religious rituals) and church activities. Symbolic gestures include dressing traditionally, behaving in a demure fashion and underplaying the egalitarianism in their relationships with their husbands.

> After going home from office I make it a point that I will talk to them for some fifteen, twenty minutes and only then I take my daughter and make her study. I make sure that I cook the dinner: at least one dish I do [in spite of having a cook] ... I start cooking around eight, eight thirty. And my maid, she cuts vegetables and gives me the spices. And my mother-in-law, but she also stands in the kitchen and she will be talking to me something, something. (Swati, 35, manager)

> I can walk for hours [in the mall] but she [my mother-in-law] can't. And also for that generation going to the mall is frivolous so our leisure activities are focused around her interests. We go to Hopcoms [a vegetable shop] or Foodworld [a supermarket]. We have some common interests: we both like exhibitions so we do things like that. I don't tend to invite people home or throw parties because I think it will burden her so I think social life with my peers is reduced. (Savita, 32, manager)

Swati's effort in cooking for her in-laws, even if the more onerous tasks are done by her maid, is part of her performance of her identity as a dutiful daughter-in-law and good homemaker. Savita's willingness to participate in her mother-in-law's interests and give her some respite from the mundane routines of housework, while curtailing her own social life, is an acknowledgement of her sense of obligation to the older woman. At a symbolic level food and dress are often put to 'expressive uses' to convey affection and gratitude (DeVault, 1999a: 54): for instance, Savita refuses to tell her mother-in-law what she would prefer to eat but eats whatever has been cooked for the day, while Swati takes her in-laws' tastes rather than her own into consideration while planning the daily menu. Women usually dress more traditionally before in-laws to show respect for their values. They tend to adopt a reserved manner that contradicts their assertive persona at work and defer to the authority of the older generation in day-to-day decisions. In this way they make the symbolic bargains necessary to win support for their professional ambitions and help with domestic duties.

> I am quite different at my in-law's place. I am very soft spoken and I don't cross my legs [a sign of casualness and disrespect towards

elders] in front of my mother-in-law. It is not like pretension or anything. The atmosphere calls for that. (Nalini, 37, manager)

Deference to tradition has been identified as an important aspect of women's participation in contemporary modernity across Asian cultures. For instance, Healey (1994) argues with respect to 'upwardly mobile' Muslim women in Malaysia that they demonstrate their modernity and Muslimness by identifying with symbols of domesticity, motherhood and orthodox Islam. The consumption of household goods and religious paraphernalia is essential to their construction of their femininity. Similarly, Indian women take pride in their role as custodians of traditions within modernity. While conformity to tradition earns them vital support within the family, they also make strategic choices as to which traditions they will follow. Anjana whose account indicates that she is self-assured and highly assertive in the workplace moderates her behaviour before her parents, asking their permission to go out not because she needs it but because it makes them feel valued:

> My parents feel it is their right to know where I am, with whom I am, what I am doing … when I decided to meet you today I had to tell them who you are, what you are doing, why this research is important. I said she is my friend's friend. She needs two hours … I have to give a lot of justifications. With my husband, I just said, 'I am going out with Nima's cousin.' It doesn't make a difference. My friends say, 'Why do you need to justify yourself so much?' but it hurts them if I don't tell them all the details. (Anjana, 33, manager)

By seeking her parents' permission Anjana reassures them that her success has not gone to her head and shows her respect and gratitude towards them by performing her identity as an obedient daughter. Thereby she increases their respectability in the extended kin-group within whose gaze her relationship with them is conducted. This is arguably the most important way of reciprocating parental care and support: the maintenance of family honour. Uma Narayan (2004) suggests that disadvantaged groups often subscribe to divergent sets of values in different contexts. The women discussed here conform to individualistic and masculinist values in the workplace while upholding traditionally feminine values at home.

It is noteworthy that men are all but absent from women's accounts of negotiating the demands of work and family life. The intergenerational exchange of domestic work and care work enable men to avoid taking an equal share in these responsibilities. It has been argued that middle class women often depend on the domestic labour of working-class women to continue in paid employment (Mulinari and Sandel, 2009). Unlike the contract between women and their domestic help which is monetized and contractual, the obligations between two generations of women in the same family need to be negotiated with tact and diplomacy and is contingent on the reciprocity of care. Indian women service the care debt that they incur with family elders by taking on additional household duties in weekends and conforming to gendered expectations in the family. Thus, to create the conditions in which they can live 'a life of one's own' (Beck and Beck-Gernsheim, 2001), they paradoxically are called upon to 'live for others'.

Conclusion

The discourse of individual choice and responsibility is fairly entrenched in many aspects of an individual's life in late modernity. However, in the workplace, this discourse is particularly strong and overlaps with that of work-life balance. In this chapter I have argued that although in theory the workplace offers flexible working practices to support employees' work-life balance, in practice this flexibility is available only to managers, who belong to the old middle class and whose families tend to be emotionally and socially more invested in their success. In contrast, women from the new middle class who are usually not on the managerial track do not have access to flexibility, and even when they do, they are not in a position to take advantage of it. Although they are more in need of support in the workplace due to the fragile nature of their support systems in their families, they are less likely to benefit from work-life-balance policies. Their accounts challenge the industry's image as a highly supportive employer for women. The 'success stories' that appear in the media and in public discourse, usually those of women in senior management positions, obscure the challenges and constraints of the vast majority of women employed in the IT industry. The latter are less likely to unequivocally endorse the 'equal opportunities employer' image of the industry.

Even when we consider the women in management who take advantage of work-life-balance policies, we find that it gives them some limited benefits at a noticeable cost to their careers and fails to appreciably reduce their dual burden. The industry's commitment to equal opportunities and diversity management does create opportunities for women to enter paid employment but does not always mitigate the effects of the masculinist culture within which they work. The language of diversity management and work-life balance might even become a means to 'invisiblize' and trivialize the professional work that women continue to carry out at home while ostensibly being available to their families. While the commitment to gender diversity in the workforce does enable women to be present in both professional and family life, it greatly diminishes their real satisfaction in both arenas. Women find themselves constantly attempting to 'get through' work in order to return home and managing the home in order to perform satisfactorily within the workplace. As Prügl (2011: 85) argues, when feminist knowledge and techniques are institutionalized (as in the corporate workplace) it has 'political consequences beyond aspirations for emancipation, liberation and an end to subordination'.

Indian women experience much of the guilt and anxiety that employed women across the world share while they face the challenges of balancing the needs of their families with the individualized values of the workplace. However, the strategies that they draw on in managing the conflict between work and home suggest that, contrary to Beck and Beck-Gernsheim's (2001) argument that we are in for a 'battle between the sexes', the family as an institution is not threatened by individualization in late modernity. Participation in paid employment might enhance women's sense of empowerment and might enable them to negotiate a better position for themselves within their families, but it does not necessarily result in individualization, nor are women necessarily seeking liberation from family ties through their participation in paid employment. Rather, it may often be the case that their participation in paid employment after marriage and childbirth further strengthens their embeddedness in reciprocal obligations within their families. A close examination of the position of middle class Indian women suggests that rather than being caught between 'living for others' and 'living a life of one's own' (Beck and Beck-Gernsheim, 1995, 2001), they subscribe to values of reciprocity and mutuality in their homes in order to succeed within the individualistic culture of the workplace.

7
Relational Reflexivity, Individual Choice and 'Respectable Modernity'

In Chapter 3 I argued that the nationalists' discourse of ideal Indian womanhood, which played a significant role in influencing women's positions in the emerging nation, has evolved into the discourse of 'respectable modernity enshrined in tradition' (Thapan, 2004). However, if we consider women's accounts of their experiences in their families and workplaces across the previous three chapters, it is evident that another discourse influences how women perceive themselves and their positions in professional and family life: that of individual choice and responsibility. I begin this chapter by examining the accounts of four research participants to see how they create narratives of self. I investigate how they draw on available cultural discourses to do so and end by discussing the interplay of the two discourses, respectable modernity and individual choice.

I use the term 'discourses' in the Foucauldian sense, as ways of ordering and perceiving the world which by their omnipresence in popular culture, in the text and talk of experts such as priests, psychologists and parents and elders influence how individuals understand and position themselves. However, while discourses influence the creation of narratives of self-identity, their influence is not always submitted to passively. Individuals 'make sense' of cultural discourses, accepting, discarding and modifying elements of the discourses to create a self-identity that is presented via a narrative of self. Given that the participants' narratives of self emerged within the context of the semi-structured research interviews, some questions arise: could these narrative accounts of self be considered 'authentic'; were they created for my benefit; what role did I have in their creation? The answers to these questions address some methodological issues in 'narrative' research.

Catherine Riessman (2008: 8) argues via Yuval-Davis that 'the identity is fluid, "always producing itself through the combined processes of being and becoming, belonging and longing to belong. This duality is often reflected in narratives of identity"'. Individuals' creation of their identities is always contextual and contingent; therefore, any attempt to capture 'an authentic identity' at any given moment is a futile exercise. This is not to argue that an authentic self does not exist, but to suggest that it shifts in relation to context. Therefore what a research interview can hope to capture is a given narrative of self in a given context. That the researcher participates in co-creating this narrative of self is undeniable. However, as I argue throughout this chapter, the self is always created in social context with reference to the gaze of others.

A more fundamental question arises as to why the participants' accounts of self are termed 'narratives'. Examining the meaning of the term narrative across different disciplines, Riessman distils the following characteristics: they consist of 'a sequenced storyline, specific characters, and the particulars of a setting'; they are 'contingent sequences which "demand the consequential linking of events, of ideas ... imposing a meaningful pattern on what would otherwise be random and disconnected"', and they are 'extended accounts of lives in context that develop over the course of a single or multiple research interviews' (quoting Salmon, forthcoming; Riessman, 2008: 5–6).

My interviews did not use the life-story approach, but they encouraged reminiscing and required interviewees to supply illustrative anecdotes or justifications for choices and decisions. During the interviews participants would often lapse into 'career narratives' reminiscent of job interviews: 'I took up "x" job and accomplished "y" after which I wanted to change to "z"' or personal narratives of 'I took decision "a" because I am a person of type "b"'. Such narratives, I would argue, come to represent a subjective sense of self or a narrative of self-identity. Not all of participants' accounts were in the nature of narratives, but the narrative of self broke through as Riessman (2008) implies, while I played my role as co-creator and coaxer (Plummer, 2001) of the narrative. My contribution to creating these narratives through the questions that I asked and the responses that I made is undeniable. However, my participation does not dilute their authenticity. While narratives that emerge in interviews are always contextual, it is arguable whether a narrative that emerges in a different context is more authentic.

Giddens (1991) argues that individuals in late modernity tend to create a reflexive biography of self, a coherent story of how and why they took certain decisions or made choices. It is possible that the preoccupation with the self in late modernity and the emphasis on the individual's responsibility of self-actualization influenced participants' accounts. My research participants have created sequenced storylines of their careers in job interviews and applications. Their exposure to what Riessman (2008: 7) describes as the 'cult of "the self"' through self-help literature, professional and personal development courses (Sathaye, 2008) and psychotherapeutic activities which focus on the individual self as a project and a responsibility might have influenced the manner in which they presented their self-construction. While Giddens' theory enables us to understand the existence of self-reflexivity in late modernity, it does not indicate how individuals actually create a sense of self, what cultural resources they draw on and how their capacity to create a self might be constrained.

Weaving narratives of self: Four case studies

The four narratives that I examine below are not necessarily representative of all the women I interviewed, nor do they represent specific 'trends' amongst interviewees' self-construction. They are simply four women of different ages and regional backgrounds who occupy distinct positions in the labour market. Two of them, Maya and Nitya, belong to the old middle class and two, Nalini and Hema, belong to the new middle class. All four are married; Nalini and Maya are also mothers. The purpose of examining their identities is to find out what sorts of discourses they draw on and how they weave together a narrative of self from cultural discourses.

Nalini

Nalini, aged thirty-seven, has been married since the age of eighteen. She lives in a nuclear household with her husband and twelve-year-old son. A legal adviser (junior manager) within the human resources team of a multinational IT company, Nalini describes herself as 'orthodox' (conservative), traditional and family oriented. A Kannada-speaking woman from a land-owning caste, she strongly identifies as South Indian referring to 'middle class South Indian families such as ours' when she wishes to underline her modesty and decorum. Though born and brought up in Bangalore, Nalini has strong links with her native village where her family still owns some land and where her in-laws still live. The death of her father when she was still in school caused financial hardship, which resulted in an early marriage and curtailed her formal education. However, she went on to acquire diplomas in social work and business administration via distance learning whilst working in personnel management at a factory and later in an IT company. Rather unusually for someone who has been in administration, she has recently entered the management cadre. While her husband has a respectable job and moderate income as a college lecturer, it is her income that enables her family to stabilize their new middle class status.

Nalini's current role requires her to investigate allegations of sexual harassment and misconduct in her company. In spite of having acquired several qualifications she describes herself as 'not ambitious or career oriented'. She asserts that she has not achieved much professionally but sees her job as a means of contributing financially to her family. Her account suggests that she values her standing in the community over her professional achievements.

> I can be a good friend to my husband and I can be a good daughter-in-law to my in-laws, a good daughter to my parents. I am the beloved sister of my brothers. I connect with people. They feel I am very approachable. If they need any help financial or otherwise or for any problems, any issues they tell me. Many people have followed my ways.

The cornerstone of Nalini's sense of self seems to be her success in maintaining family relationships and fulfilling family responsibilities. Work plays an important role in her life, but mainly as a way of enhancing and supporting her familial responsibilities: acting as a helpmate to her husband, bringing worldly wisdom and insights into the relationship and relieving him of some of his responsibilities as a breadwinner in a somewhat unstable economy, bringing up her son in a rapidly changing culture and having the capacity to support family members who are in need.

Nalini's income plays a vital role in the family's financial stability as her husband's income as a college lecturer is not enough to support their middle class lifestyle. While she acknowledges that the money she earns 'plays a parallel role' to 'love and moral support', enabling her husband to make larger investments, take financial risks and save for her son's education, she also attempts to underplay the importance of her contribution with repeated comments such as 'I am from a financially sound background', or 'I don't need the money.' Thus we see a tension between her need to affirm her own contribution and to maintain her husband's dignity as the main breadwinner. She attempts to resolve this tension by declaring that her husband is 'the finance minister of the house' who manages her income as he has a better head for figures and 'no bad habits' [spendthrift tendencies or addictions]. In this manner the family's respectability is maintained.

In addition, Nalini values her profession for the exposure it creates to the changing globalized world, which she believes, makes her a well-informed parent, capable of making the right decisions for her son. Nalini is strongly invested in her identity as a mother and deeply concerned about her son's academic, social and emotional development. She speaks of preparing special meals for him, taking him to swimming classes and other sports activities and supervising his school work. To enhance his decision-making skills she takes his views into account when buying products or planning holidays.

> We discuss a lot in front of my son – he is aware of things that is happening at home and many times we ask his decision also. I think this open discussion at home may not be entertained in families where women are not working. ... Many times I fight with my husband. I feel that might be negatively affecting my kid. Then immediately I will speak with my kid. This was the reason I fought with him. Not for anything big. [It's not that] I'm not okay with him [his father]. I'll update him [my son] so that way he feels, 'If my parents fight also they had some reason to fight it out, not for some silly reason.' Otherwise it will really have some wrong effect on their future life. That's what I read: if [their] parents fight, later in their family life they won't speak at all with their partners.

Nalini's concern with her son's emotional development indicates strong influence of the notion of the child as a delicate project (Beck and Beck-Gernsheim, 1995), to be undertaken with a serious sense of purpose and careful planning. While these attitudes suggest that in her role as a mother she draws on the discourse of individual choice and responsibility, her 'rational' attitude to parenting may also be associated with the discourse of respectable modernity.

In addition to her role as wife and mother, Nalini takes pains over her religious duties. Her economic independence and professional identity have not affected her traditionalism.

> Whatever we do outside the family, that's fine, but ultimately you have do something else for yourself and your family ... Otherwise, I don't see any challenge for the family to get along or run. I really

observe [follow] all the festivals: Mahashivratri, Ugadi … whatever my mother was doing: weekly visit to temples, doing pooja [rituals], meditations. I really want to continue that atmosphere … when we are at home the atmosphere should be very cool [peaceful].

While Nalini sees herself as the custodian of traditions within the family, this traditionalism is not incompatible with assertiveness in public. She uses tact and firmness in dealing with peers, government officials and colleagues, attributing her success in handling people to her ability to remain decorous while firmly asserting her position. This decorum and dignity are the visible markers of her spirituality which preserve her reputation and virtue in public (Chatterjee, 1989).

I look eye-to-eye contact and show complete professionalism. With my boss also we discuss all these issues [of sexual harassment] together. I never show my shyness; it's part of life. I am very, very firm. I really bifurcate [between professional and personal] things. When I talk to you, I can demarcate – 'When it's professional I should talk to Nalini and when it is personal only to this level I can talk to her.' – 'How is your family? How are your kids?' That is all … My husband also has confidence [in me]. If I take a drop with a male colleague also he knows me [for] what I am.

Nalini indicates that she preserves her honour and chastity through assertiveness and decorum. By her own account, her reputation as a dignified and assertive woman allows her to enter conventionally masculine spaces such as the shop floor of a factory without fear of harassment or dishonour. To prevent sexual harassment she feels that boldness should be combined with modesty, particularly by refraining from 'loose talk' (sexual innuendo, personal references). Underscoring her ability to draw clear boundaries she otherizes women who are overly approachable or timid.

Nalini's narrative brings together a number of seemingly contrasting values: assertiveness and modesty, boldness and reticence, traditionalism and progressiveness, materialism and spiritualism. She chooses to emphasize one value over another depending on the context in which she is creating her identity. Her boldness, her materialism and outward progressiveness, her interaction with men and her participation in the seamier side of the public world (investigating sexual harassment for instance) are necessitated by the economic exigencies of globalization. This 'superficial progressiveness' is 'only skin deep' (Sunder Rajan,

1993: 133) and is outweighed by a more 'genuine' self which is deeply embedded in tradition, religiosity and family relationships. Women such as Nalini might outwardly accept unequal gender relations but recognize the value of assertiveness outside the home and economic independence within it to prevent the balance of power from tipping completely against them. By a discerning use of tact and assertiveness, they communicate their own power and capacity for self-determination.

Maya

Although she is the same age as Nalini, Maya's account of herself is radically different, as is her background and education. Unlike Nalini she does not identify herself in caste terms and only mentions her regional and linguistic identity (Bengali) in passing. She lives in a nuclear household with her husband and two-year-old son, but her parents who recently moved to Bangalore from Lucknow to help her with childcare live nearby. Maya who is from an urban, metropolitan background belongs to the old middle class, grew up in Mumbai (Bombay) where she did her schooling and went on to acquire an MBA degree from a well-reputed institution. A senior manager in a multinational IT company, she describes herself as very focussed on her career.

> I grew up in Bombay so I lived there for a very long time but I moved to Bangalore around '95. I wanted to be in information technology companies so it made sense for me to move out of Bombay which had limited scope in that area. So, spoilt brat that I was, I actually came here without my parents' knowledge [laughter]. My dad was then in Lucknow, my mother and sister had gone there for a vacation and I sneaked out and came to Bangalore to do some interviews without letting them know … I guess I was trying to see – going out and trying my own thing. I also believed that Lucknow was not the place for me to go. Interestingly, that was also the perspective of my parents. My mother was extremely ambitious for me. My father has always guided me. I was one of the few who at that age got career counselling. It's common place today. It wasn't so common place that time.

Maya recounts her 'rebellious' and 'spoilt' behaviour with much delight, setting up her identity as a self-determined woman. However, it is apparent that she had more opportunities than Nalini beginning from her school days. She shows some awareness of these privileges by acknowledging that her father (a private sector employee who had the cultural resources to understand the value of career counselling) supported her career. In her account she frequently acknowledges that her parents and husband 'are extremely ambitious for me, more than I am frankly, for myself'.

When we met, Maya was approachable but business-like, seeming to position me as a feminist scholar who was researching policy initiatives for women in the workplace and made a point of declaring her opposition to such policies quite early in the interview. 'I am a bit worried that people will see us as this special class of people who need special attention because that is something that takes away from your achievements.' The underlying message seemed to be that her success is the result of her own effort and hard work rather than any concessions on account of being a woman. She distances herself from women who demand concessions, arguing that they 'cut a sorry figure' and diminish the achievements of those like herself who succeed without concessions.

While Nalini's sense of self came from otherizing women who lacked dignity and assertiveness in public, Maya creates her identity by otherizing women who ask for concessions in the workplace (see previous chapter). Her own childcare solution is to leave her son with her parents through the day, and, when pressured at work, through the night, because of which she can 'manage like a man' (Wajcman, 1998) and does not need to seek those 'additional workplace supports' that she strongly opposes. Maya's argument of individual responsibility for individual choices may be contradicted when she attributes her success to her husband's support and her parents' decision to relocate to Bangalore to help her with childcare, but to acknowledge that other women may not have similar support (and may therefore need it from the workplace) would undermine her own narrative of self-determination.

Maya's account of herself as a career-orientated woman does have some ambivalences created partly by motherhood and partly by unfinished dreams:

> I wanted to be a wildlife photographer but other than subscribing to national geographic I have done nothing about it.

Or, later in the interview,

> I would like to perhaps branch out on my own and be a consultant but I'm afraid I'll just get lazy and stay at home.

In addition her family has invested so much in her identity as a 'career woman' she feels compelled to live up to their expectations:

> They see me like this, I think it would be hard for them to accept my shifting gears.

As Bauman (1998) argues, a life of unlimited choices, paradoxically, tends to erode individual autonomy since no choice is ever completely made. Every option exists only to exclude the possibility of other or better options. In this context the neoliberal discourse of choice and responsibility can place a heavy burden on individuals, but this burden is compounded in the case of Indian women by the tension between their commitment to individualism and their embeddedness in family relationships.

This embeddedness is evident in the manner in which individual achievement is used to augment family honour. While Nalini preserves her family's prestige by underplaying her own financial contribution and emphasizing her husband's respectability, Maya positions her family as progressive and open-minded when she calls attention to how they encouraged her as a 'girl child to be financially independent'. These inputs seem to inspire a sense of obligation, which is repaid through achievement, thus increasing the family's honour and social standing. Maya's success becomes evidence of her family's modernity and progressiveness. When she argues that women like herself are responsible for their career choices and the consequences of those choices, she locates her narrative within the discourse of individual choice and responsibility. However, her own individual project of self, as Giddens (1991) terms it, cannot be undertaken without the inputs of family who themselves have a stake in her success.

Like Nalini, Maya is deeply concerned about her child, and given the demands of her job, she experiences a high degree of guilt and anxiety about her role as a mother. Maya brings a certain business-like attitude and vocabulary to her maternal responsibilities and concerns for her child's health, education and development.

> Right now, I'm putting together a list of things such as taking him to museums and play parks and such like. And, you know drive to it because he does need some of those inputs.

The business jargon 'drive' that translates as 'taking responsibility for a goal' might suggest a managerial approach to childcare (Hochschild,

2003) but masks the anxiety associated with it. Maya had recently decided to take her son out of playschool because of his tendency to frequently pick up infections from his classmates but was highly conflicted about her decision. Otherwise confident and self-assured, the only time when she questions her capabilities is with regard to motherhood.

> I took the call because I couldn't see him suffer any more. I just sort of felt that what happened because of whatever reason and he used to hate going to school, by the way. He said he wouldn't go out to play! He got so angry with us! And he's just a two-year-old. He's like, 'I won't!' He wouldn't go and play with other kids. Now I said two-year-olds are not supposed to be very social people anyway, but you at least expect him to go out and play with the swing and the slide in the break. I said, 'Forget it! I don't want to send him to school.'

Later in the interview,

> Sometimes you feel you're taking a decision in a vacuum. You wish you know more people with kids or with similar issues, but I just don't have the time to connect up. I don't have the time to hang out around a playground every day of the week to find out from other mums whether what I'm doing is the only way to do it or if there is another way.

Maya shares the guilt of other 'working mothers' when she leaves her child behind with her parents (see Wajcman, 1998; Hochschild, 1989; Pocock, 2003). For all the support of her family, she is, like many other professional women, fairly alone in dealing with her anxieties and guilt since she does not have a support network of friends in similar situations.

While Maya and Nalini are very different in their class backgrounds, opportunities and relationship with their careers, they are united in their commitment to responsible mothering and their anxiety for their children. They share similar concerns and tend to draw on discourses of responsible mothering which could arguably be called a subset of the individual choice and responsibility discourse. However, responsible motherhood has been an essential feature of discourses on Indian womanhood since the nationalist period (Chatterjee, 1989) and continues to be important within the discourse of respectable modernity. In their separate analyses, both Oza (2006) and Thapan (2004) suggest that in media discourse women's ability to make discerning choices is closely connected with their capacity as mothers. Therefore it could be argued that the two discourses, that of individual choice and respectable modernity, work together to create high and somewhat unattainable mothering expectations for women. With this understanding of the interplay between the two discourses, we turn to the narratives of women who are not yet mothers.

Hema

> Situation forced me to work. As and when you have an experience you will have a confidence, that's what I learnt. Education is not a prime priority in your life. Without that also you can survive, that's what I learnt. Because so many people who are my friends, who have completed postgraduation also, they are still in their own backlogs. They are struggling to earn money and survive in the industries. I've already settled; it's a good decision I took not to study. Initially I was back-logging. I didn't have a graduation [degree] all the stuff. It was little tough but today I'm almost settled.

Twenty-six-year-old Hema had been married for nearly two years at the time of the interview. She was living on her own and working as administrative assistant in a multinational company. She and her husband had set up a nuclear household not far from her parents' home, but on getting a good job offer from a company in Hyderabad he had moved there. Although their financial situation required them to live separately for some months, she hoped the situation would be temporary. Hema grew up in Bangalore in a 'conservative Brahmin family' where she was seldom allowed to leave the house alone. Both her parents had clerical jobs in the public sector and managed on a modest income until her mother was diagnosed with cancer a year before Hema graduated from school. With two younger sisters and a father financially ruined by his wife's illness, Hema decided to take up a fax operator's job in a private company whilst pursuing her BSc via distance learning. She is doing a part-time MBA and is highly satisfied with the choices she has made.

> My mom had a uterus cancer, so much of money was flowing to it and my sisters also – my second sister, she was falling sick very often so my father couldn't manage the expenses and we were on loans ... I didn't wanted to write CET [the test for entering engineering college] but my father forced me because I was good at academics. I was not very good but 75–85% I used to get, so that's how I landed

up writing CET and he [her father] was so desperate for me to join to engineering but I didn't feel like going, being an elder daughter. If it was a son definitely it would have been his responsibility to take care of them right? So I said, 'why can't daughter?' ... I was about to support my parents' family. After marriage I still continued to do that. I wanted my parents to live comfortable life.

As the main breadwinner in her family, Hema challenges upper caste notions about women's positions in their families and the transience of daughters within the parental home. While she employs the vocabulary of individual choice when describing her decision to give up formal education in favour of a job, the sense of family obligation underlying the decision is evident from her remarks. While she might have been motivated by the need to maintain family honour before me, a stranger, in presenting the decision as a personal one, she takes pride in support-ing her parents and earning an income. 'I'm the first person to have bought a car in the family as a girl and it's been really proud.'

Her initial position as a young girl from a financially vulnerable family entering the job market without skills or formal education left her vulnerable to harassment, exploitation and redundancy. She tried to overcome the threat of sexual harassment by avoiding interactions with men, but this was not always possible. Although she recounts two instances where harassment led her to give up her job, her eagerness to learn new skills enabled her to grow in her career. With help and advice from her fiancé (now her husband) she gradually grew more confident both in her interactions and in her work and currently considers herself a competent professional.

Hema's marriage also challenges conventional notions of arranged marriages. She describes herself as having been 'promised' to her hus-band, Shekar, in her childhood, via an arrangement between their fathers, which is unusual in contemporary India. Unfortunately, his parents were killed in an accident soon after he joined university, leav-ing him financially crippled and forcing him to give up his studies. While the similarity in their situations brought Hema and Shekar closer together, it made her mother re-think the wisdom of marrying her daughter into a family that was as bankrupt as her own.

My mother, you know, after that incident, she started looking out to other persons because Shekar was not well settled. I was very particular [about marrying only Shekar]. I had a fight [with her]; I had to give some interviews [meet potential bridegrooms]. Yeah,

I used to go. I was going and telling all the fellows, 'See, I have a love, this was fixed when I was born. I can't change my mind.' I used to go and explain to ... For past twenty years [I was committed to Shekar], suddenly if you want me to change how can I change? The last and final one [interview] – it was in 2004. It came up to marriage – direct marriage. He [the prospective groom] was in USA – software engineer and he wanted to marry and just fly off – just in fifteen days. He came, saw me and he said, 'Okay we'll do the marriage in temple and we'll just finish it off.' I was so scared. It was happening so fast. I was very particular that I don't want to run and go off and disturb my parents. All I wanted is I want to marry Shekar but in front of my parents with their blessings. So that time I had a little tough time ... Because that fellow didn't have a father, only mother who was in US with him – they were very well settled. He's the only son so mamma wanted something like that [for me so that I could be comfortably settled]. I mean I don't blame her. As a mother she will think in that way. Then finally we fought and ... My uncle helped me a lot. So then, we just got engaged, myself and Shekar ... My uncle did one counselling [spoke to my parents on my behalf] – till today I don't know what he said; may be a two- two-and-half-hour discussion with my parents. Finally they concluded that if I got, get engaged with Shekar, they will not proceed further with the other fellow.

In her account Hema constructs her identity as a caring and dutiful daughter. She believes that her duty extends beyond meeting her parents' material needs. Her job enables her to contribute to their financial well-being while her daily calls and visits and her close involvement in family affairs such as securing a job for one of her sisters and finding a suitable groom for the other enable her to give them 'moral supports and emotional supports also'. However, her commitment to them did not prevent her from refusing to let them arrange her marriage. In spite of her concern for them or perhaps because of it she was able to negotiate space for her own wishes.

At the same time Hema's account of her marriage confounds the categories of arranged marriages and marriages of choice. On the one hand one could argue that she married by choice and exercise her right to self-determination. On the other hand considering that her marriage had been arranged from her cradle, it is questionable whether she did make an independent choice even after engaging in considerable negotiation with her parents. While she was able to carry her point through, it was not without help from her extended family. Parallels may be drawn between her account and Nitya's account below.

Nitya

Nitya is twenty-seven years old and was married for seven months at the time of the interview. She identifies herself as a South Indian and is married (by choice) to a North Indian;[1] the couple live in a joint household with her husband's parents. A qualified (chartered) accountant, Nitya works as a financial analyst (executive) with a multinational communication technology firm. The daughter of a doctor father and a school teacher mother, she shares the old middle class value for achievement and professional success. Her pride in being part of a global company and optimism about the future could make her a poster-child for globalization and its benefits for women. Nitya derives a strong sense of fulfilment from paid work and believes that 'this is the time for me to concentrate on my career rather than on cooking, attending weddings and following the traditions'. She describes her experience in the first job as follows:

> It was a very good learning experience, especially [in] the first six months: how you talk, the confidence and the way you dress. Lot of things I had to learn. I made some of my good friends when I was with ——— [name of company] It was great! You know, every day there was something! When you meet a client or when you analyse everything is in terms – I had never attended a conference call – when you log in and different things. Everything was new – things like you can get coffee as many times as you wish. We had individual cabins. You have a desk at twenty and then you have a phone and you're making presentations and meeting the CFOs – something really great.

The perks which seemed at first to have a magical quality, making her feel grown-up and responsible, have become familiar four years later but haven't completely lost their appeal. She still enjoys travelling as part of the job and makes sure she has time for sightseeing when the company sends her abroad. While she has clear professional goals, including starting her own consultancy, Nitya has also begun to invest in her identity as a wife, daughter-in-law and future mother.

Of her marriage, Nitya cautiously mentions that her in-laws were 'sceptical about our relationship'. Since she also shares that 'it took a good two years to convince them' to consent to the marriage, it is likely that the opposition to the marriage was quite strong. However, Nitya shows no resentment towards them and takes pains to win their approval.

> When they compliment me on – I never used to wear saris [but now I do]. They're very impressed that I have taken the extra trouble to wear a sari and come for a [family] function. I can wear anything I want; it's just that they compliment [me]. When I get up in the morning and help my mother-in-law, they notice that and they say that I am taking an extra initiative. If I keep my room clean, she says, 'You manage everything'. So I know they are noticing it and I feel very happy.

Having challenged the authority of the older generation, by electing to marry against their wishes, Nitya now takes pains to re-establish traditional authority structures and conform to the normative expectations associated with her position as a daughter-in-law. In another part of her account, she indicates that her parents approved of the match but were unwilling to let the marriage take place until her husband's parents also gave their consent. She also argues that the approval of other family members, such as aunts and uncles, while not essential, was important to her decision. Like Hema she sought approval and sanction for her choice even while she expressed her autonomy.

Nitya's respect for her in-laws is indicated by her refusal to criticize them before me, a stranger, and her efforts to dress and behave in a way that wins their approval. These efforts might be necessitated by her somewhat vulnerable position as a young bride from another community, but two factors are in her favour: her willingness to adapt to their lifestyle and her professional qualifications. Her in-laws' affection might be influenced by their desire to reciprocate Nitya's generosity in overlooking their past conduct and repair their relationship with their son, but they are also likely to be influenced by the need to augment family prestige. By underlining her professional qualifications which (by Nitya's account) exceed that of other women in their family, her in-laws gain in status and construct an identity as modern family who support their women in professional life.[2]

> When my father-in-law introduces me he says this is my daughter-in-law, she is a chartered accountant … she is doing the same job as my son. It feels so good!

From this remark one might infer how closely Nitya's professional and personal identities are interlinked and how her in-laws' pride in her professional success is connected to her sense of self. As in Maya's case Nitya's professional achievements not only raise her own self-esteem but also augment her family's prestige. The self that emerges in this context is not constructed through autonomous choices but in relationship with her family and wider community and through their collective gaze. Her personal identity as a daughter-in-law is enhanced by her professional identity as a chartered accountant in some contexts and in conflict in others. Nitya is aware of this conflict, and while she currently has no ready solution to it, she acknowledges that it will be exacerbated by motherhood.

> May be I was able to put in any amount of hours; before getting married I had no restriction of, I didn't have any responsibility. Right now I do have – I need to have a cut off. I will work from nine to five but after that I want time at home. If I am never present and I'm always very involved with my work, if I don't make a contribution from my side I can't get into – I can never be the daughter-in-law.

The four narratives of self that are discussed are fairly distinct; yet some similarities may be drawn. Firstly women's presence in paid employment does not necessarily lead to individualization. Rather they remain bound within the normative expectation of their positions in their families. Even when women's incomes are vital to the family's security they take pains to prevent their contribution from threatening existing authority structures based on gender and seniority. Individual choice whether in the area of professional life or marriage is always made in a structural and cultural context. Both Hema and Nitya might have made martial choices against the wishes of their families (whether parents or in-laws), but they took pains to gain the consent and approval of their families.

While professional success does not absolve women from the duties associated with their positions as daughters and daughters-in-law, professional and personal identities are not always in conflict. Maya's and Nitya's families might not be dependent on their incomes, but their professional identities augment their families' honour. All four narratives suggest that an individual's sense of self is rarely disconnected from her family's identity and prestige in the community.

While women's professional experiences may be appreciated for this reason within their families and while it might make them more well-informed, responsible mothers, the time competition between work and family life creates other dilemmas. Women feel the need to make a choice between effectiveness in one or the other domain. This is a choice that is constraining rather than liberating, a factor that Giddens does not account for in his concept of reflexivity.

Divergent and overlapping discourses

The two discourses, that of respectable modernity enshrined in tradition (respectable modernity for short) and individual choice and responsibility (individual choice for short), are evident in the above narratives. Here I revisit some key tenets of these discourses not only drawing from the four narratives above but also pointing out how they might be embedded in the accounts of other interviewees as well.

The discourse of respectable modernity

From the narratives above we might argue that the discourse of respectable modernity is fairly influential in women's construction of their self-identities. While it is most prominent in Nalini's narrative, it is evident in Maya's, Nitya's and Hema's self-constructions as well, especially in their embeddedness in family life, which is a key feature of the discourse. The discourse of respectable modernity charges women with maintaining and servicing family ties and holds them responsible for preserving and transmitting traditions. While many women accept this responsibility for the affection and appreciation that it brings them, they tend usually to take a broader view of tradition and selectively to preserve only those traditions that are celebratory and inclusive. Jyoti who feels responsible for passing on traditions to her daughter, nevertheless, refuses to follow traditions that are divisive or demeaning to others:

> We had this function for my daughter's birthday. My mother-in-law has a sister who became a widow last year, so my mother-in-law asked me, 'Do you have a problem with her coming?' because usually they don't allow widows to come [to ritual occasions] especially in the first year [after becoming widowed]. I said [that] I don't have a problem. Why exclude somebody? (Jyothi, 29, executive, mother)

The discourse of respectable modernity does not place women only within the home. Just as education was valued in the nationalist period for the broader outlook it enabled women to achieve, which enhanced their abilities as wives and mothers, today professional employment is believed to play the same role. In Nalini's account I discussed how her professional role makes her a well-informed mother. Anita suggests that it creates greater equality and companionship in marriage:

> Somewhere I understand his stresses more because I am at the work-place and am answerable to someone. So I can appreciate the fact that he's also got work-related stress. There are days when we're both stressed and it becomes a very pressure cooker–like situation, but we are able to appreciate what the other person is going through. You're able to connect better because of that ... much better than my father and mother were able to connect because she wasn't earning. ... I think your husband values you a little more intellectually as an equal person because you have your own occupation. (Anita, 32, manager, mother)

Just as educated women were believed to be a more suitable companion to her husband in the nationalist period, so are 'working women' valued for their intelligence and ability to empathize with men's concerns in the period of globalization. Anita indicates that the common experience of facing workplace stress draws her and her husband closer as companions and equal partners and creates positive role models for children. However, their participation in paid employment does threaten their virtue which needs to be protected by appropriate behaviour. Any appearance of overfriendliness with men or vulgarity is subjected to harsh criticism and ridicule.

> The way you dress, wearing a loud jazzy kind of colour or a short skirt and a plunging neckline; the way you communicate with people ... There are people who get too friendly with colleagues ... people take as much liberty with you as you give them. So if you're talking to a colleague and you ask too many personal questions or crack all kinds of jokes and things like that, that gives people a lot of liberty. You have to choose whom you give this liberty and to whom you don't. (Rupa, 28, manager, married)

Elsewhere I have discussed how the reputations of women who experience harassment at work are scrutinized to find out if they have transgressed the norms of appropriate female behaviour (Belliappa, forthcoming). Within the discourse of respectable modernity women are expected to clothe themselves in cloak of tradition which preserves their virtue as they engage in public life. Elements of modernity are incorporated into women's identities, which as Sunder Rajan (1993) argues, are only 'skin-deep'. Rupa's criticism of her colleagues becomes a means of otherizing them and constructing herself as a respectable woman who engages confidently with modernity. A similar observation is made by Smita Radhakrishnan (2011) in her research of female IT professionals wherein she suggests that they embody 'respectable femininity' in their globalized workplaces. I have tried to argue above that respectable modernity runs much deeper as it informs not only women's professional identities but also their very sense of self and becomes a means for evaluating others.

The discourse of individual choice

> I think every individual answers the question (of how important their work is) for themselves. Yes! Because the importance of work to me and the importance of work to you are so different. You look at it from your perspective. I don't know. I haven't been in your shoes; you know what it means from your perspective and therefore what you need to put into it or not put into it. If I am working for fashion money every day then I will just put in that amount of effort to take the money and buy myself new clothes, but if that's not my driver, then something else is my driver, then I will hold myself differently. So I believe that the question is yours to answer. (Maya, 37, manager, mother)

Maya's remarks echo those of Subroto Bagchi, the IT industry leader quoted in Chapter 5. Both suggest that commitment to work is an individual decision and attribute a woman's lack of commitment to feminine concerns like 'making pickle' (Bagchi in Chapter 5) or 'fashion' (Maya, above). The rhetoric of individual choice, however, allows them to appear non-judgemental while essentially trivializing feminine pursuits and overlooking women's more serious need to care for their families or the strong premium that is put on personal grooming and self-care in the IT workplace, which might require women to spend a portion of their income on clothes and 'fashion'. More importantly it sets up decisions about work commitment, income and personal and professional stability as individual problems outside the influence of gendered and class-based structures. Christina Scharff (2011) argues in her discussion of young British and German women that in neoliberal society individual effort is deployed to overcome structural barriers, thereby excluding the possibility of collective identification and action (as in the case of the feminist movement). Consider Maya's position articulated above in relation to this exchange from a focus group:

Jyothsna: In terms of balancing personal and professional life, has the company helped? What policies have helped and what hasn't helped?

Beena: I'm doing a very bad job of balancing it. I'm pathetic, which is why I go through these guilt pangs, saying, 'May be I should just quit.' But then every time I talk of quitting then I get talked out of it in office because then you're not being fair to yourself because now you're feeling guilty about doing this to your family. If you quit then you're not being fair to yourself which in a way is true and really ...

Sarah: I'm finding it difficult to – especially now, I'm doing these mad hours. ... I guess what's helped a lot because I have a lot of these late-night calls, it is I have the flexibility of working from home if I want to. The flip side is that you end up doing all of these odd hours but I've made a decision. During the week I will work all these crazy hours; Saturday, Sunday, I'm not downloading my email. And I find it helps so during the week ... I'm getting frustrated and angry because it's not taking me up the ladder – may be it should take me somewhere.

Upasna: I think for me, I've started growing to strike a balance between the personal and the professional ... I'll have to be more strong to take that on, you know, so really I'm growing to strike that balance.

(Upasna, 28, married, executive; Sarah, 36, married, manager; Beena, 30, married, manager)

Systemic issues that influence women's capacity to create a work-life balance include the division of labour between the sexes, the undervaluing of unpaid work, the demands of client-servicing roles, the 'identity affirming' nature of (certain) jobs (Lewis, 2003: 349) and the construction of the ideal worker as the one who works longest. Yet in response to my question on organizational policies, Upasna, Sarah and Beena all analyse their own capacities to create work-life balance rather than company policies. They do not question their positions in the global economy that undermine their ability to take advantage of work-life balance policies. Although Sarah indicates her disappointment in not being rewarded adequately, her only resistance to the long-hours culture is to avoid working on weekends. Like the women interviewed by Scharff (2011), they might recognize the systemic factors that constrain them but choose their own individualized solution to them: growing stronger and more mature, as Upasna suggests. They tend to overlook the need for structural and cultural changes in order to create a work-life balance (Lewis, Gambles and Rapoport, 2007).

Giddens argues that individuals are free to construct their own biography via a series of choices; however, these choices are not always liberating. As Lash (1993) suggests, the idea of individual choice and responsibility takes the form of a choice that sometimes has a coercive influence on individual action. The discourse puts high pressure on women as it does not allow them to 'fail' on either front: professional or personal. It suggests that the right 'blend' of choices would lead to success in both family life and professional life. However, as Maya's account indicates this 'right blend' is so delicate a balance that it is rarely achieved, and few participants claim to be happy with their current blend of choices. Women's choices and associated responsibilities are often in conflict partly due to contradictory expectations in the wider culture and partly due to the difference between personal desires and social norms. Therefore, choices are often made with a sense of ambivalence and are rarely final.

> I leave the house at six thirty in the morning as soon as my son wakes up and he sleeps at seven thirty in the evening, so if I don't go home at five thirty, I haven't seen him the whole day. You feel, 'Is it worth it?' But spend one day at home [and] you realize 'I can't do this'. I've educated myself and I enjoy – And I'm so passionate about what I do. I just love what I do, so why not? (Swarna, 31, manager, mother)

In addition to the conflict between the responsibility she feels towards herself to realize the investment of time, money and effort in her education and her responsibility to her son, Swarna's remarks indicate a conflict between her need for self-actualization through work and her need to be available to her son and enjoy the experience of motherhood. The notion that each aspect of one's life is a means of self-expression is part of the discourse of individual choice. The career becomes part of the individual's attempts to create a meaningful self-identity, to answer the question: 'who am I?' However, motherhood is also perceived as a means of self-expression, a choice and a joy. Therefore, Swarna is, as Bauman

(1998) argues, 'doomed to choice' with neither choice offering complete satisfaction. Women in particular are called upon to choose between self-expression through motherhood and self-expression through a career unlike men whose paternal responsibilities necessitate the pursuit of professional success and financial stability.

With the expansion of marital choices contemporary Indian women are expected to take greater responsibility for the consequences of their choices, especially if these have been made against parental advice as Geetika, Nitya and Jaya did. Nitya who married against her in-laws' wishes feels a strong responsibility to make a success of her marriage, which means not only servicing the marital tie as Geetika and Jaya do (see Chapter 4) but also strengthening her relationship with her in-laws. While the exchange of compliance for respect and protection may be part of the patriarchal bargain (Kandiyoti, 1988), it is expressed in the vocabulary of individual choice. Even when choices are made within normative cultural expectations such as having children within a few years of marriage, women construct them as an individual decision and therefore an individual responsibility.

> I try and do the maximum justice to my work and my child ... simply because I think I should earn my living if the company is paying me and I should do justice to my daughter, because I made a decision to have a child, so it's not dictated by anything or anyone else but primarily by what I feel. (Anjali, 30, manager, mother)

Anjali's choice to have a child involved the concurrence of her husband and may have been influenced by cultural norms regarding the 'right' age for motherhood and the expectations of the extended family. However, she conceptualizes it as an individual decision. This puts the responsibility for the child's upbringing almost completely on her shoulders, constructing the involvement of the child's grandparents and father as a favour rather than a shared responsibility. Thereby the discourse of individual choice and responsibility, instead of emancipating women from structural constraints and defined social identities as Giddens (1991) suggests, further strengthens these identities in addition to increasing their guilt and anxiety.

Williams (2000) argues that in modern 'egalitarian' marriages, wives are no longer bound to comply with husbands because of inferior status, but decisions are taken from the point of view of what's best for everyone's (especially children's) emotional well-being. So women 'choose' full-time motherhood or part-time work as the best option for their families' happiness and to meet their own emotional needs as wives and mothers, but this is not a choice that is freely engaged.

Conclusion

While the discourse of respectable modernity differs in notable ways from the nationalist discourse of ideal womanhood, it has evidently evolved from the former. For instance, it continues to charge women with maintaining the spirituality of the home and of the culture in general, indicating that women's spirituality protects them from the seamier side of public life. In contrast, the discourse of individual choice and responsibility is a late modern phenomenon that could be attributed to the individualization of the labour market and the increasing popularity of neoliberal ideas amongst middle class Indians.

The two discourses may ostensibly conflict with each other in terms of their emphasis on collective versus individualist values, but a closer investigation suggests that they can often reinforce each other as in the case of motherhood. The discourse of respectable modernity upholds motherhood as a sacred duty while that of individual choice and responsibility turns it into a highly demanding project which needs to be undertaken with care and discrimination. The widespread cultural belief that the quality of the mothering can have a deep impact on the child's development further reinforces the message of the two discourses.

Another way in which the two discourses seem to interact is that the vocabulary of individual choice and responsibility is often used to describe collective responsibilities. Women may speak of choosing to show respect for tradition and deference to elders rather than being forced to do so. Without disputing the authenticity of these claims we can conclude that they draw both on the discourse of respectable modernity which positions them within the home and the discourse of individual choice which encourages them to take responsibility for their own well-being when they emphasize their traditionalism and defer to their elders. They make a strategic decision to conform to traditional normative standards in order to strengthen their positions within their families.

While the two discourses discussed above are not the only discourses available to Indian women, they are certainly predominant in interviewees' constructions of self. Women draw on different elements of these discourses (and presumably on others) to create narratives of self that are distinct in many respects though they might have some commonalities. They exercise agency in choosing which elements of the discourses to incorporate in creating a self that is shifting and contingent on circumstances. Their narratives suggest that even within a seemingly narrow constituency such as Indian middle class women, individuals have differential access to resources for the reflexive construction of self. Old middle class women such as Maya and Nitya have a broader range of choices in constructing a narrative of self due to their greater access to cultural capital than new middle class women like Nalini and Hema who have less access to cultural capital. Their experiences suggest that the concept of 'reflexivity' needs to account for differences in access to resources for reflexive self-construction.

Conclusion: The Collective Project of Self

A sizeable number of middle class women in India have benefitted from the expansion of the private sector following India's integration into the global economy, gaining unprecedented incomes and enjoying much greater freedom of mobility than earlier generations. As earlier chapters have argued their prominence in public and professional life is recognized not only by their families but also by the media and popular culture. However, this recognition fails to take into account the many challenges associated with their position. Many of the jobs created in the transnational private sector in general and the IT industry in particular are fairly low skilled and associated with minimal growth opportunities but are coveted because of the high incomes that they offer in comparison with companies based in India or servicing the Indian market.

Moreover, they have little incentive to build a lasting relationship with the labour they hire. As Bauman (2000) argues, the contemporary period is one of 'liquid capitalism'. The integration of the world's economies enables transnational corporations to move from one region to another in search of conducive labour markets and cheaper production centres, but labour tends to remain fixed to a given location. India's integration into the global economy might have enhanced job opportunities, but it has also made the national economy more vulnerable to a global recession or downturn. Although several multinational companies have entered India, and local companies have established transnational links, their ability to move at short notice keeps such corporations beyond the reach of unions and employee associations. They may offer luxurious work environments and high salaries but demand very high levels of commitment whilst offering little security. At present Indian workers are valued because of their knowledge of English, their perceived capacity for hard work and their ability to engage with the West. However, as new markets develop across the world, these assets might cease to be unique. Middle class women who have benefitted from private sector jobs also experience greater job insecurity compared with previous generations.

In Chapters 5 and 6 I argued that the private sector in general and the IT industry in particular regularly reiterate their commitment to gender diversity. The institutionalization of feminist goals under the banner of diversity management has benefited some women in the IT industry. However, not all women benefit equally. Women in junior and middle managerial positions tend to gain some benefits from policies of positive discrimination at the workplace but also face gender stereotypes that owe their origin partly to the wider culture of gender discrimination outside the organization and partly to the backlash against positive discrimination. Male employees might resent the flexibility given to their female colleagues or ridicule the latter's family commitments.

Women remain the outsiders within a work culture that operates around the industrial notion of the organizational man whose wife takes care of the domestic and caring responsibilities. They also remain excluded from male networks and informal associations which influence professional success. Due to their association with care work they tend to remain concentrated in roles that are associated with fewer growth opportunities. The few women who reach senior management do so because they rarely seek benefits such as extend maternity leave or flexi time since it interferes with their career growth. They are usually able to avoid doing so because of the high levels of support that they receive from their parents or in-laws, especially in the area of childcare. However, although their professional success is closely related to their ability to negotiate support within their families, they tend to evaluate it in individualistic terms, that is, as an outcome of individual effort.

Women across all levels in management (senior, middle and junior) tend to be from the old middle class. They are in a position to mobilize their inherited cultural capital for professional success. This cultural capital might include fluency in English, cosmopolitan attitudes and ability to mingle with people across regional, linguistic and cultural boundaries. Women in administrative and support functions who are not on the management track tend to be from new middle class families and rarely inherit the kind of cultural capital required to enter the management track. At the workplace, they are rarely given flexibility in work schedules and the option of working from home. Even on the rare occasions when they work from home, their home environments do not afford them the privacy to do so effectively. In most cases, their families cannot or are unwilling to support their professional commitments by providing substitute care at home. Thus it happens that those women who are most in need of support at the workplace are least likely to benefit from it.

In spite of these difficulties, women from new middle class backgrounds continue in paid employment in order to anchor their families more firmly in the middle class. They appreciate the income that they are able to earn within the transnational market and the financial security that it affords their families. From the research one might raise questions about the private sector's purported commitment to meritocracy, arguing with Stevi Jackson (2008) that individualization of the labour market produces both choices and constraints (see Chapter 2) for women. It is clear that both class and gender influence women's career growth as much as individual effort.

However, the discourse of individual choice and responsibility can obscure the influence of these structural and cultural factors in creating the conditions within which they work. The neoliberal construction of the autonomous self-determined individual precludes the possibility of women coming together to recognize shared problems or take collective action. In Beck and Beck-Gernsheim's (2001) words they tend to seek 'individual biographical solutions to systemic contradictions'. As employees they are expected to negotiate their work hours individually with their managers. Those who are able to articulate their 'worth' to the company are more likely to succeed in negotiating work-life balance strategies.

Women therefore tend to become alienated from each other: women in managerial positions (primarily from the old middle class) do not seem to appreciate the challenges faced by administrative staff (primarily from the new middle class). While companies do promote 'women's forums' these forums do not take a stand against organizational policy since they are constituted by the organization itself, suggesting that the institutionalization of feminist goals can sometimes undermine their effectiveness.

Women's pursuit of professional success is not just motivated by personal goals but is also a way of meeting family obligations. These obligations include repaying the emotional and financial investments that their parents make in their education by contributing to their family's income and its prestige. A son or daughter working in the transnational economy enables both old and new middle class families to strengthen and consolidate their middle class position and even move closer to the elite. In supporting their daughters' and daughters-in-law's careers in the transnational economy, families are motivated by love, pride and the desire to 'do and display' their modernity. In addition, they gain access to consumer goods, real estate and comfortable lifestyles. Therefore, as long as women's careers and incomes do not threaten traditional authority structures based on age and seniority, parents and in-laws support them by taking over some of their caring obligations, thus enabling women to conform to the individualistic values of the labour market.

When women mobilize family support in fulfilling their caring obligations, they incur a care debt which they meet by conforming to traditional gendered norms and values. Contrary to Beck and Beck-Gernsheim's (2001) assertion that women are torn between living for others and living a life of one's own, Indian women tend to live for others in order to live a life of their own. Women exchange conformity in one arena to gain choices in another, carefully calibrating how they might create room for their own agendas within the framework of traditional norms and gendered values. In this manner, they attempt to negotiate for and barter power within their families and the labour market to expand their choices.

The period of reflexive modernity has given middle class women in India an increased capacity for negotiation within the families and greater choice in marriage. For instance marriages are increasingly based on similarities of class, professional status and personal compatibility; caste, though important, is being interpreted more broadly in marriage and is replaced by regional and linguistic endogamy. However, while women might be encouraged to participate in arranged marriage decisions alongside their parents, or even to make marriages of choice, once the decision is made, the marriage is enacted in the gaze of the family and community. Therefore women might 'choose' to recreate more traditional gender relations in the marriage and may disguise evidence of egalitarianism in the relationship before their parents and extended families. While couples might have a fairly egalitarian relationship to begin with, the birth of children might oblige them to conform to more traditional gendered roles. The tendency for women to marry men who are older, more educated or from a better class position might further undermine the equality in the marital relationship. These indications of inequality in marital ties are largely overlooked in Giddens' theory of pure relationships. Mulinari and Sandel (2009) argue that the pure relationship as Giddens describes it is 'a relationship without children'; it may well be a relationship without the elderly, without parents, in-laws or other kin whose expectations may influence the marriage.

When women make what might be seen as individualized choices in marriage they try to ensure the success of these choices through the deployment of tact and diplomacy and by selectively conforming to traditional norms. If successful, these choices result in personal happiness, social acceptance and continued protection within the kin-group. If individualistic choices do not pan out, women may be left vulnerable and exposed. They may then have to contend with the threat of harassment, financial insecurity and emotional despair. In these cases many women attempt to re-establish the patriarchal bargain (Kandiyoti, 1988) and regain protection within their natal and marital families by conforming to traditional norms.

Thus the nature of Indian women's reflexivity is considerably different from the kind described in the reflexive modernity thesis. While they do create reflexive biographies of self, their reflexivity is socially grounded and contextualized by the specificities of history, ethnicity and culture. Tokita-Tanabe (2003) argues that women create their sense of self within the social gaze. Taking inspiration from both Tokita-Tanabe (2003) and Mead (1934), we might argue that Indian women's reflexivity incorporates the gaze of others: family, friends and community. Not only do they incorporate the gaze of others into their construction of self, but they also conduct all their relationships within the gaze of others, including their relationships with their partners (see above and in Chapter 4) and their relationships with their parents (see Chapter 6). They choose to conform to traditional gendered norms to augment the prestige of their parents and in-laws. Since women are seen to be the repositories of the honour of two families, their natal family and their marital family, members of both families are active participants in the creation of a woman's individual self. Therefore, in the Indian context the self may be seen as not just an individual project but a collective project, one in which families have considerable stake.

The self that emerges within this socially constituted reflexivity is shifting and relational. It shifts in relation to context and also in relationship with others. Women make choices about which aspects of their identities to emphasize in different contexts. For instance they might sometimes mobilize the more traditional aspects of their identities to work in masculinized environment without fear of harassment or slander or they might conform to traditions at home to garner support for their professional goals. At other times they might need to behave in a more individualized manner to be accepted within the labour market, masking their commitment to their families before colleagues and managers.

Women exercise their reflexivity within the structural inequalities of gender, class, ethnicity, race and geography, which enable or limit their choices. Adkins argues following Lash that due to differential access to resources, some groups emerge as reflexivity's winners at the cost of other groups who emerge as reflexivity's losers. Without seeing winning and losing as water-tight compartments, it may be argued that all individuals gain some advantages from reflexivity whilst also incurring some losses. Even within a fairly specific category such as middle class Indian women, we find that old and new middle class women have differential access to resources for constructing a reflexive project of self. Not only economic position, but also family circumstances, education and social background can limit women's access to resources.

An important argument of this book is that while choices may have expanded in reflexive modernity, individuals do not become empowered as a consequence. Instead individual choice and responsibility is a discourse that paradoxically influences individuals' choices in reflexive modernity. It not only can encourage women to negotiate for personal agendas and desires within structural or cultural constraints but can also pressurise them into taking responsibility for their choices whilst masking how those choices might be limited. As in the case of other discourses (such as that of respectable modernity), it has the capacity to emancipate as well as to constrain individual action. Moreover, these two discourses are not necessarily the only discourses available to Indian women – others might also exist within the broader culture. While discourses exert some pressure on women and constrain their choices, as Scot Lash would argue (see Chapter 2), they exercise agency in deciding which elements of the discourses to draw on and in what manner to combine them, thus creating a self that might share some common characteristics with others but is also fairly unique.

The research in this book suggests that reflexivity is historically situated. In the case of Indian women it is situated in conditions of postcolonialism and within a history of cultural and political domination by Europe. Therefore, individual women are influenced in their reflexive construction of self by both a fascination with and a resistance to European culture. Given India's recent emergence as an economic power, their reflexivity is also influenced by a new-found confidence in the nation's cultural heritage. In their construction of self they emphasize their 'Indianess' as well as their familiarity with 'world culture'.

Historical circumstances also have another role to play in Indian women's construction of their self-identities. Since the colonial period, women are believed to represent the nation's progress and its modernity, a position that women themselves have participated in co-constructing since it earns them considerable prestige. They are conscious that their participation in professional life and in public discourse indicates the nation's modernity and therefore take pride in their presence in both arenas. However, as women in a postcolonial nation they are also positioned as custodians of tradition. Women participate in this construction of themselves since it gives them certain advantages: honour, prestige and a degree of safety in public life. Although they discard customs that they deem as superstitious or bigoted, many women take responsibility for preserving and recreating traditions. Following traditions associated with their childhood, such as celebration of religious feasts or festivals, keeping religious fasts and re-enacting religious rituals, enables them to create a sense of continuity with the past in the face of globalization. Religious occasions also bring respite into their somewhat routinized lives, and engaging with spirituality enables them to deal with the stress and uncertainty of life in contemporary modernity. Women's reflexive construction of self is thus marked by their position as bearers of their families, and the culture's spirituality.

The accounts of women discussed in this book indicate that reflexivity occurs within a framework of unequal relationships of power. They suggest that although individual agency plays a role in constituting an individual's reflexivity, it is also influenced by the social gaze and by available cultural discourses. The concept of reflexivity needs to be understood in terms of social, historical and cultural contexts. By reframing the concept to take into account these contexts and the nuance of class, gender, ethnicity and other structural factors, we might take a small step in the direction of creating a theory of reflexive modernity that is more nuanced and complex than what is currently in existence. More empirical research is needed to create a complex understanding of contemporary modernity that is sensitive to the intersections of gender, class, geography and ethnicity. As we focus the lens on different communities and cultures within the Global South, as well as on non-mainstream groups in the North, new patterns will emerge, which will not rely on one grand theory or broad thesis, but will need to consist of a kaleidoscope of small-scale, localized theories which are limited in their scope and context but sharply focused in their conclusions. It is in the hope of collaboratively building this kaleidoscope of research that I offer this book to other scholars.

Notes

1 Setting Out to Study Class and Gender in Contemporary India

1. *Pandita* is a title given to a female scholar (often a scholar of ancient Sanskrit texts) – a rare achievement for a woman of the 19th century.
2. The Tata group of companies launched the 'Nano', a car that initially cost only one lakh, that is, one hundred thousand rupees, in 2009 (at the time of this conversation it was not yet on the market) (See The Economist, 2008).

3 The 'New' Indian Middle Class Woman

1. The National Council for Applied Research (NCAER) India is a highly reputed economic research institution in India. Surveys and reports produced by the NCAER are extensively used by the government and industry to inform policy decisions.
2. Jayawardena, 2002, with regard to Srilanka; Chatterjee, 1989, with regard to India; Pollard, 2005, with regard to Egypt.

4 Individualism and Responsibility: Women's Relationships Within Their Families

1. The term is coined by M. N. Srinivas (1959) to describe the practice of suppressed castes attempting to emulate the lifestyles, customs and practices of the upper castes in an attempt to gain higher status.

5 Women's Relationships with Paid Work in the Transnational Economy

1. Of late private colleges with better infrastructure and much higher fees than government-aided colleges have grown, but the government colleges continue to enjoy high enrolment.
2. Forward community refers to those (traditionally privileged castes) who do not enjoy the benefits of affirmative action such as reservation of places in university and government jobs. The 'forward castes' (upper castes) often express resentment against the policy of reserving positions in universities for students from the depressed castes and oppose such reservations on the grounds of 'meritocracy'.

6   Managing Paid Employment and Family Life

1. Fredrick Taylor, a late 19th-century mechanical engineer, is credited with the modern management practice of dividing tasks in a manner that allows the maximum possible work to be accomplished in the minimum possible time. Taylor's ideas were widely implemented, regulating the work of blue-collar workers in the steel and automotive industries. The notion of Taylorization is associated with strict regimentation of tasks to ensure maximum efficiency even at the cost of alienating workers.

7   Relational Reflexivity, Individual Choice and 'Respectable Modernity'

1. Although she gives clearer details of her and her husband's linguistic identities, revealing them would make her more identifiable.
2. Since I did not speak directly with Nitya's in-laws this interpretation is based on what she reports; however, her participation in creating this family identity is apparent from her remarks.

References

Adams, M. (2003) 'The Reflexive Self and Culture' *British Journal of Sociology* 54 (2): 221–238.

Adams, M. (2006) 'Hybridizing Habitus and Reflexivity: Towards an Understanding of Contemporary Identity?' *Sociology* 40 (3): 511–528.

Adkins, L. (2000) 'Objects of Innovation: Post-occupational Reflexivity and Re-traditionalisations of Gender' in S. Ahmed, J. Kilby, C. Lury, M. McNeil, and B. Skeggs (eds), *Transformations: Thinking Through Feminism.* New York and London: Rutledge.

Afshar, H. (1989) 'Gender Roles and the *"Moral Economy* of Kin" among Pakistani Women in West Yorkshire' *New Community* 15 (2): 211–225.

Agnes, F. (1994) 'Women's Movement within a Secular Framework: Redefining the Agenda' *Economic and Political Weekly* 29 (19): 1123–1128.

Agnihotri, I. and Mazumdar, V. (1995) 'Changing Terms of Political Discourse: Women's Movement in India, 1970s–1990s' *Economic and Political Weekly* 30 (25 October): 1869–1878.

Ahmed, L. (1992) *Women and Gender in Islam: Historical Roots of a Modern Debate.* New Haven and London: Yale University Press.

Alexander, L. (2007) 'Women on Top!' *The Hindu Metro Plus* [online]. Available at http://www.hindu.com/mp/2007/03/08/stories/2007030800730100.htm [Accessed 14/10/08].

Aneesh, A. (2006) *Virtual Migration: The Programming of Globalization.* Durham: Duke University Press.

Appadurai, A. (1996) *Modernity at Large: Cultural Dimensions of Globalization.* Minneapolis: University of Minnesota Press.

Awaya, T. (2003) 'Becoming a Female Citizen in Colonial Kerala' in A. Tanabe and Y. Tokita-Tanabe (eds) *Perspectives from Asian and the Pacific.* Kyoto and Melbourne: Kyoto University Press and Trans Pacific Press.

Bagchi, S. (2007) 'The Board Room of the Future & the Role of Professional Women'. Speech delivered at the NASSCOM IT Women Leadership Summit in Bangalore 12/12/2007. Available at http://www.mindtree.com/subrotobagchi/articles-by-subroto/ [Accessed 28/3/2013].

Basi, J. K. T. (2009) *Women, Identity and India's Call Centre Industry: Close Calls and Hang Ups.* London and New York: Rutledge.

Bauman, Z. (1998) *Globalization: The Human Consequences.* New York: Columbia University Press.

Bauman, Z. (2000) *Liquid Modernity.* Cambridge: Polity Press.

Bauman, Z. (2001) *The Individualized Society.* Cambridge: Polity Press.

Beck, U. (1992) *Risk Society: Towards a New Modernity.* London: Sage.

Beck, U. (1999) *What Is Globalization?* Cambridge: Polity Press.

Beck, U. (2000) *The Brave New World of Work.* Cambridge: Cambridge University Press.

Beck, U. and Beck-Gernsheim, E. (1995) *The Normal Chaos of Love.* Cambridge: Polity Press.

Beck, U. and Beck-Gernsheim, E. (2001) *Individualization: Institutionalized Individualism and its Social and Political Consequences*. London: Sage.

Beck-Gernsheim, E. (2002) *Reinventing the Family: In Search of New Lifestyles*. Oxford: Polity.

Belliappa, J. (2006) 'Our Palms are Not Meant Only for Henna: Agency, Tradition and Modernity in Contemporary Bollywood Films' *The International Journal of Diversity in Organisations, Communities and Nations* 6 (5): 9–16.

Belliappa, J. (forthcoming) 'She Was Very Outgoing': Sexual Harassment and Appropriate Female Behaviour in The Indian Information Technology Industry' *Travail, Genre et Societies (Work, Gender and Societies)*.

Béteille, A. (1993) 'The Family and the Reproduction of Inequality' in Uberoi, P. (ed.) *Family, Kinship and Marriage in India*. New Delhi: Oxford University Press.

Béteille, A. (2001) 'The Social Character of the Indian Middle Class' in Ahmad, I. and H. Reifeld (eds) *Middle Class Values in India and Western Europe*. New Delhi: Social Science Press.

Bhagat, R. (2007) 'The Changing Indian Woman' *The Hindu Business Line* [online]. Available at http://www.thehindubusinessline.com/2007/10/03/stories/2007100350530900.htm [Accessed 19/07/08].

Bhambra, G. (2009) *Rethinking Modernity: Postcolonialism and the Sociological Imagination*. Palgrave Macmillan.

Bhavnani (1994) 'Tracing the Contours: Feminist Research and Feminist Objectivity' in Afshar, H. and Maynard, M. (eds) *The Dynamics of Race and Gender: Some Feminist Interventions*. London and Bristol: Taylor and Francis.

Brannen, J. and P. Moss (1991) *Managing Mothers: Dual Earner Households after Maternity Leave*. London: Unwin Hyman.

Bulbeck, C. (1998) *Reorienting Western Feminisms*. Cambridge: Cambridge University Press.

Business Week (2005) 'India's New Worldly Women' [online]. Available at http://www.businessweek.com/magazine/content/05_34/b3948530.htm?campaign_id=spr_rediff_india [Accessed 12/08/08].

Caplan, P. (1985) *Class and Gender: Women in India*. London: Tavistock.

Chakravarti, U. (1989) 'Whatever Happened to the Vedic Dasi? Orientalism, Nationalism and a Script for the Past' in Sangari, K. and S. Vaid (eds) *Recasting Women: Essays on Colonial History*. New Delhi: Kali for Women.

Chang, K. and Song, M. (2010) 'The Stranded Individualizer under Compressed Modernity: South Korean Women in Individualization without Individualism' *Sociology* 61 (3): 539–564.

Chatterjee, P. (1989) 'The Nationalist Resolution of the Women's Question' in Sangari, K. and S. Vaid (eds) *Recasting Women: Essays on Colonial History*. New Delhi: Kali for Women.

Connell, R. (2008) *Southern Theory: The Global Dynamics of Knowledge in Social Science*. Crow's Nest: Allen and Unwin.

Crompton, R. (2006) *Employment and the Family: The Reconfiguration of Work and Family Life in Contemporary Societies*. Cambridge: Cambridge University Press.

Das, G. (2000) *India Unbound: From Independence to the Global Information Age*. New Delhi: Penguin.

Das, V. (1993) 'Masks and Faces: An Essay on Punjabi Kinship' in Uberoi, P. (ed.) Family, *Kinship and Marriage in India*. Delhi: Oxford University Press.

Deb, S. (2003) 'Womancipation' *Outlook* 24/11/2003, Special Issue.

Deshpande, S. (2003) *Contemporary India: A Sociological View*. New Delhi: Penguin.

DeVault, M. L. (1999) *Liberating Method Feminism and Social Research*. Philadelphia: Temple University Press.

DeVault, M. L. (1999a) 'Comfort and Struggle: Emotion Work in Family Life' *The Annals of American Academy of Political and Social Science* 561 (1): 52–63.

Dex, S. (2003) *Families and Work in the 21st Century*. York: Joseph Rowntree Foundation.

di Leonardo, M. (1987) 'The Female World of Cards and Holidays: Women, Families, and the Work of Kinship' *Signs* 12 (3): 440–453.

Dube, L. (2001) *Anthropological Explorations in Gender: Intersecting Fields*. New Delhi: Sage.

Dumont, L. (1993) 'North India in Relation to South India' in Uberoi, P. (ed.) Family, *Kinship and Marriage in India*. Delhi: Oxford University Press.

Dyuti, A. (1998) 'Shackling Ambition' *Deccan Herald*, Bangalore. Available at http://www.cscsarchive.org/MediaArchive/news.nsf/(docid)/5475FECFC1071 922652569410040C8A6 [Accessed 28/04/08].

Economy Watch (ca. 2009) 'FDI in India's IT Industry' [online]. Available at http://www.economywatch.com/india-it-industry/fdi.html [Accessed 27/02/09].

The Economic Times (2011) 'India's middle-class population to touch 267 million in 5 yrs'. Available at http://articles.economictimes.indiatimes.com/2011-02-06/news/28424975_1_middle-class-households-applied-economic-research [Accessed 26/9/11].

Favero, P. (2005) *India Dreams: Cultural Identity among Young Middle Class Men in New Delhi*, Stockholm Studies in Anthropology 56. Stockholm: University of Stockholm.

Fernandes, L. (2006) *India's New Middle Class: Democratic Politics in an Era of Economic Reform*. Minneapolis: University of Minnesota Press

Finch, J. and Mason, J. (1993) *Negotiating Family Responsibilities*. New York and London: Rutledge.

Fleetwood, S. (2007) 'Why Work-Life Balance Now?' *International Journal of Human Resource Management* 18 (3): 387–400.

Foucault, M. (1976/1990) *The History of Sexuality: An Introduction, Volume 1*. New York: Vintage Books.

Folbre, N. and J. A. Nelson (2000) 'For Love or Money – Or Both' *The Journal of Economic Perspectives* 14 (4): 123–140.

Forbes, G. (1996) *Women in Modern India. The New Cambridge History of India: Vol. 4*. Cambridge: Cambridge University Press.

Friedman, T. (2005) *The World Is Flat: A Brief History of the Twenty-First Century*. New York: Farrar, Strauss and Giroux.

Fuller, C. and Narasimhan, H. (2007) 'Information Technology Professionals and the New-Rich Middle Class in Chennai (Madras)' *Modern Asian Studies* 41 (1): 121–150.

Fuller, C. and Narasimhan, H. (2008) 'Companionate Marriage in India: The Changing Marriage System in a Middle-Class Brahman Subcaste' *Journal of Royal Anthropological Institute* 14 (4): 736–754.

Gaikwad, R. (2010) 'Need for Feminists to Reclaim Ambedkar seen' in *The Hindu* [online]. Available at http://www.thehindu.com/news/national/article78658ece [Accessed 26/10/12].

Giddens, A. (1990) *The Consequences of Modernity*. Cambridge: Polity Press.

Giddens, A. (1991) *Modernity and Self-Identity: Self and Society in the Late Modern Age*, Cambridge: Polity Press.

Giddens, A. (1992) *The Transformation of Intimacy: Sexuality, Love and Eroticism in Modern Societies*, Cambridge: Polity Press.

Giddens, A. (1999) *Runaway World: How Globalization is Reshaping Our Lives*. London: Profile Books.

Giddens, A. (2002) *Runaway World: How Globalization is Reshaping Our Lives*. London: Routledge.

Grover, S. (2010) 'Lived Experiences: Marriage, Notions of Love, and Kinship Support amongst Poor Women in Delhi' *Contributions to Indian Sociology* 43 (1): 1–33.

Guillaume, C. and Pochic, S. (2009) 'What Would You Sacrifice? Access to Top Management and the Work–life Balance' *Gender, Work and Organization* 16 (1): 14–36.

Guha, R. (ed.) (2010) *The Makers of Modern India*. New Delhi: Penguin.

Gupta, D. (2000) *Mistaken Modernity: India between Two Worlds*. New Delhi: HarperCollins.

Hattery, A. (2001) *Women, Work and Family: Balancing and Weaving*. Thousand Oaks: Sage.

Hayami, Y. Tanabe A. and Y. Tokita-Tanabe (eds) (2003) *Perspectives from Asian and the Pacific*. Kyoto, Melbourne: Kyoto University Press and Trans Pacific Press.

Healey, L. (1994) 'Modernity, Identity and Construction of Malay Womanhood' in Gomes, A. (ed.) *Modernity and Identity: Asian Illustrations*. Victoria: La Trobe University Press.

Heaphy, B. (2007) *Late Modernity and Social Change: Reconstructing Social and Personal Life*. London: Rutledge.

Heelas, P. (1996) 'Introduction: Detraditionalization and its Rivals' in Heelas, P., Lash, S. and P. Morris (eds) *Detraditionalization: Critical Reflections on Authority and Identity*. Cambridge, MA and Oxford: Blackwell.

Hobsbawm (1983) *The Invention of Tradition*. Cambridge: Cambridge University Press.

Hochschild, A. R. (1997) *The Time Bind: When Work Becomes Home and Home Becomes Work*. New York: Henry Holt.

Hochschild, A. R. (2003) *The Managed Heart: Commercialization of Human Feeling*. Berkley: University of California Press.

Hochschild, A. R. (with A. Machung) (1989) *The Second Shift: Working Parents and the Revolution at Home*. New York: Penguin.

ILO (2008) 'ILO EAPEP' (Estimate and Projections for Economically Active Population) for 2008' in ILO Laborsta Table E5. Available via: http://laborsta.ilo.org [Accessed 26/9/11].

Irwin, S. (2005) *Reshaping Social Life*. Abingdon: Rutledge.

Jackson, S. (2008) 'Materialist Feminism, the Pragmatist Self and Global Late Modernity: Some Consequences for Intimacy and Sexuality' in Gunnarsson, L. (ed.) *GEXcel Work in Progress Report Volume III. Proceedings from GEXcel Theme 1: Gender, Sexuality and Global Change*. Lingkoping: Centre of Gender Excellence – GEXcel.

Jackson, S. (2010) 'Self, Time and Narrative: Re-thinking the Contribution of GH Mead' *Life Writing* 7 (2): 123–136.

Jafferlot, C. and van der Veer, P. (2008) 'Introduction' in Jaffrelot, C. and P. van der Veer (eds) *Patterns of Middle Class Consumption in India and China*. New Delhi: Sage.

Jamieson, L. (1999) 'Intimacy Transformed? A Critical Look at the 'Pure Relationship' *Sociology* 33 (3): 477–494.

Jayawardena, J. (2002) 'Cultural Construction of the "Sinhala Woman" and Women's Lives in Post-Independence Sri Lanka' PhD. York: University of York.

Kakar, S. (1988) 'Feminine Identity in India' in Ghadially, R. (ed.) *Women in Society: A Reader*. New Delhi: Sage.

Kandiyoti, D. (1988) 'Bargaining with Patriarchy' *Gender and Society* 2 (3): 274–290.

Karnik, K. (2008) 'Transforming IT and Rural India' on *The National Association of Software and Services Companies (*NASSCOM*) Emerge Blog* [online]. Available at http://blog.nasscom.in/emerge/2008/06/10/transforming-it-and-rural-india [Accessed 26/9/11].

Karve, I. (1967/1993) 'The Kinship Map of India' in Uberoi, P. (ed.) *Family, Kinship and Marriage in India*. Delhi: Oxford University Press.

King, A. (1999) 'Legitimating Post-Fordism: A Critique of Anthony Giddens' Later Works' *Teleos* (115): 61–77.

Krishna, A. and Brihmadesam, V. (2006) 'What Does it Take to Become a Software Professional?' *Economic Political Weekly* 41 (30): 3307–3314.

Lash, S. (1993) 'Reflexive Modernization: The Aesthetic Dimension' *Theory Culture & Society* 10 (1): 1–22.

Lewis, S. (2003) 'The Integration of Paid Work and the Rest of Life. Is Post-industrial Work the New Leisure?' *Leisure Studies* 22 (October) 345–355.

Lewis, S., Gambles, R. and Rapoport, R. (2007) 'The Constraints of "Work-Life Balance" Approach an International Perspective' *International Journal of Human Resource Management* 18 (3): 360–373.

Liddle, J. and Joshi, R. (1986) *Daughters of Independence*. London and New Delhi: Zed Books and Kali for Women.

Madan, T. N. (1993) 'The Structural Implications of Marriage Alliances in North India: Wife-Givers and Wife-Takers among the Pandits of Kashmir' in Uberoi, P. (ed.) *Family, Kinship and Marriage in India*. Delhi: Oxford University Press.

Mani, L. (1989) 'Contentious Tradition: The Debate on Sati in Colonial Indian' in Sangari, K. and S. Vaid (eds) *Recasting Women: Essays on Colonial History*. New Delhi: Kali for Women.

Mankekar, P. (1999) *Screening Culture, Viewing Politics*. Durham and London: Duke University Press.

McRobbie, A. (2009) *The Aftermath of Feminism: Gender, Culture and Social Change* London, Thousand Oaks and New Delhi: Sage.

Mead, G. H./Morris, C. (1934/1967) *Mind, Self, and Society: From the Standpoint of a Social Behaviorist*. Chicago: University of Chicago Press, 2009.

Mitchell, W. and E. Green (2002) '"I Don't Know What I'd Do without Our Mam": Motherhood, Identity and Support Networks' *The Sociological Review* 50 (4): 1–22.

Mohanty, C. T. (1984) 'Under Western Eyes: Feminist Scholarship and Colonial Discourses' *Boundary* 12 (3): 333–358.

Morris, C. W. (ed.) (1962) *Works of George Herbert Mead Vol. 1: Mind, Self, & Society form the Standpoint of a Social Behaviourist*. Chicago and London: University of Chicago Press.

Mulinari, D. and Sandell, K. (2009) 'A Feminist Re-reading of Theories of Late Modernity: Beck, Giddens and the Location of Gender' in *Critical Sociology* 35 (4): 493–507.

Nair, J. (2011) 'Indian Historiography and its "Resolution" of Feminists' Questions' in Ghosh, A., Guha-Thakurta, T. and J. Nair (eds) *Theorizing the Present: Essays for Partha Chatterjee*. New Delhi: Oxford University Press.

Nandy, A. (1983) *The Intimate Enemy: Loss and Recovery of Self under Colonialism*. Oxford: Oxford University Press.

Narayan, U. (2000) 'Essence of Culture and a Sense of History: A Feminist Critique of Cultural Essentialism' in Narayan, U. and S. Harding (eds) *Decentering the Center: Philosophy for a Multicultural, Postcolonial, and Feminist World*, Bloomington: Indiana University Press.

Narayan, U. (2004) 'The Project of Feminist *Epistemology*: Perspectives from a *Nonwestern* Feminist' in Harding, S. (ed.) *The Standpoint Theory Reader*. London, New York: Routledge.

NASSCOM (2009) Releases Indian IT Software and Services – FY09 Performance and Future Trends. Available at http://www.nasscom.in/Nasscom/templates/NormalPage.aspx?id=55739 [Accessed 26/9/11].

NASSCOM (2010) NASSCOM Impact Study 2010 Executive Summary. Available at http://www.nasscom.in/upload/68924/Impact_Study_2010_Exec_Summary.pdf [Accessed 26/9/11].

NASSCOM (2010a) Promoting a culture of diversity and inclusivity at work. Available at http://www.nasscom.in/Nasscom/templates/NormalPage. *aspx*?id=60361 [Accessed 26/9/11].

National Council of Applied Economic Research (NCAER) (2005): *The Great Indian Market* [pdf]. New Delhi: NCAER in association with *Business Standard*. Available at http://www.ncaer.org/downloads/AnnualReports/AnnualReport_2005.pdf [Accessed 14/10/08].

National Informatics Centre (2009) The Ministry of Labour Annual Report 2008–09. Available at http://labour.nic.in/annrep/annrep0809/Chapter-11.pdf [Accessed 26/9/11].

Nayare Ali (2006) 'Hi Tech Women' *Asian Age* [online]. Available at http://www.nasscom.in/Nasscom/templates/NormalPage.aspx?id=49604 [Accessed on 27/06/08].

Netting, N. (2010) 'Marital Ideoscapes in 21st-Century India: Creative Combinations of Love and Responsibility' *Journal of Family Issues* 31: 707–726.

Nongbri, T. (1993) 'Gender and the Khasi Village' in Uberoi, P. (ed.) Family, *Kinship and Marriage in India*. Delhi: Oxford University Press.

Obbo, C. (1989) 'Sexuality and Economic Domination in Uganda' in Yuval-Davis, N. and F. Anthias (eds) *Woman, Nation and State*. Basingstoke and Hampshire: Macmillan.

Oldenberg, V. T. (2010) *Dowry Murder: Reinvestigating a Cultural Whodunit*. New Delhi: Penguin.

Oza, R. (2006) *The Making of Neoliberal India: Nationalism, Gender, and the Paradoxes of Globalization*. New York and London: Routledge.

Padke, S. (2003) 'Thirty Years On: Women's Studies Reflects on the Women's Movement' *Economic and Political Weekly* (25 October), 38 (43): 4567–4576.

Pandita Ramabai and M. Kosambi (1888/2000) 'The High-Caste Hindu Woman' in *Padita Ramabai Through Her Own Words: Selected Works*. Oxford University Press.

Padmanabhan, P. (2008) 'IT Women Want Gender-Sensitive Policies' *Cybermedia India Online Limited* 25 January 2008 [online]. Available at http://www.ciol.

com/news/feature/it-women-want-gender-sensitive-policies/25108103099/0/ [Accessed on 28/02/09].

Patel, V. (1988) 'Emergence and Proliferation of Autonomous Women's Groups in India: 1974–1984' in Ghadially, R. (ed.) *Women in Society: A Reader*. New Delhi: Sage.

Plummer, K. (2001) *Documents of Life 2: An Invitation to Critical Humanism*. London, Thousand Oaks, and New Delhi: Sage.

Pocock, B. (2003) *The Work/Life Collision: What Work Is Doing to Australians and What to Do About It*. Sydney: The Federation Press.

Poggendorf-Kakar, K. (2001) 'Middle-Class Formation and the Cultural Construction of Gender in Urban India' in Ahmad, I. and H. Reifeld (eds) *Middle Class Values in India and Western Europe*. New Delhi: Social Science Press.

Pollard, L. (2005) *Nurturing the Nation: The Family Politics of Modernizing, Colonizing and Liberating Egypt, 1805–1923*. Berkeley: University of California Press.

Posner, J. (1992) *The Feminine Mistake: Women, Work, and Identity*. New York: Warner Books.

Prügl, E. (2011) 'Diversity Management and Gender Mainstreaming as Technologies of Government' *Politics & Gender* 7 (1): 71–89.

Puri, J. (1999) *Women, Body, Desire in Post-Colonial India: Narratives of Gender and Sexuality*. London and New York: Routledge.

Radhakrishnan, S. (2011) 'Gender, the IT Revolution and the Making of a Middle-Class India' in Ray, R. and Baviskar, A. (eds) *Elite and Everyman: The Cultural Politics of the Indian Middle Classes*. London, New York and New Delhi: Routledge, pp. 193–219.

Radhakrishnan, S. (2011a) *Appropriately Indian*. New Delhi: Orient Black Swan.

Ramalingam, A. (2007) 'IT's a Woman's World' *The Sunday Times of India*. (11/03/2007): 2.

Ramusack, B. N. and Sievers, S. (1999) *Women in Asia: Restoring Women to History*. Bloomington and Indianapolis: Indiana University Press.

Rathore, T. and Sachitanand, R. (2007) 'Winning Them Over: It's an Equal World' *Business Today*. 17 June 2007 [online]. Available at http://archives.digitaltoday. in/businesstoday/20070617/careers.html [Accessed 2/03/09].

Ray, R. and A. Baviskar (2011) *Elite and Everyman*. New Delhi: Routledge.

Rege, S. (1998) 'Dalit Women Talk Differently: A Critique of Difference and Towards a Dalit Feminist Standpoint Position' *Economic and Political Weekly* (31 October), 33 (44): WS39–WS46.

Rich, E. (2005) 'Young Women Feminist Identities and Neo-liberalism' *Women's Studies International Forum* 28: 495–508.

Riessman, C. K. (2008) *Narrative Methods for the Human Sciences*. Los Angeles and London: Sage.

Rosenthal, C. J. (1985) 'Kinkeeping in the Familial Division of Labor' *Journal of Marriage and the Family* 47 (4): 965–974.

Runté, M. and Mills, A. J. (2004) 'Paying the Toll: A Feminist Post-structural Critique of the Discourse Bridging Work and Family' *Culture and Organization* 10 (3): 237–249.

Säävälä, M. (1998) 'The Hindu Joint Family: Past and Present' in Parpola, A. and S. Tenhunen (eds) *Changing Patterns of Kinship and Family in South Asia: Proceedings of an International Symposium on the occasion of the 50th Anniversary of India's Independence held at the University of Helsinki 6 May 1998*. Helsinki: The Finnish Oriental Society.

Sathaye, S. (2008) 'The Scientific Imperative to be Positive: Self-reliance and Success in the Modern Workplace' in Upadhya, C. and A. R. Vasavi (eds) *In an Outpost of the Global Economy: Work and Workers in India's Information Technology Industry*. New Delhi: Routledge, pp. 136–161.

Scharff, C. (2011). 'Disarticulating Feminism: Individualization, Neoliberalism and the Othering of "Muslim women"'. European Journal of Women's Studies 18 (2): 119–134.

Scrase, T. and Ganguly-Scrase, R. (2009) *Globalisation and the Middle Classes in India: The Social and Cultural Impact of Neoliberal Reforms*. London and New York: Routledge.

Shah, A. M. (1973) *The Household Dimension of the Family in India: A Field Study in a Gujarat Village and a Review of Other Studies*. New Delhi and Berkeley: Orient Longman and University of California Press.

Shenoy, P. (2003) 'Retention of Women Managers in the InfoTech Industry – A Qualitative Study', Women, Information and Communication Technology in India and China: International Forum, Hawke Research Institute for Sustainable Societies.

Shinde, T. (1882/2010) 'A Comparison of Men and Women' in Guha, R. (ed.) *The Makers of Modern India*. New Delhi: Penguin.

Shinde, T. (2011) 'A Comparison of Men and Women' in Guha, R. (ed.) *The Makers of Modern India*. New Delhi: Penguin/Viking.

Skeggs, B. (2004) *Class, Self and Culture*. Routledge, London: New York.

Sklair, L. (2001) *The Transnational Capitalist Class*. Oxford: Blackwell.

Smart, C. (2007) *Personal Life: New Directions in Sociological Thinking*. Cambridge: Polity Press.

Smart, C. and Shipman, B. (2004) 'Visions in Monochrome: Families, Marriage and the Individualization Thesis' *The British Journal of Sociology* 55 (4): 491–509.

Spivak, G. (1999) *A Critique of Postcolonial Reason: Toward a History of the Vanishing Present*. Harvard: Harvard University Press.

Srinivas, M. N. (1959) 'The Dominant Caste in Rampura' *American Anthropologist*. New Series, 61 (1): 1–16.

Srinivas, T. (2002) 'A Tryst with Destiny' in Berger, P. L. and S. P. Huntington (eds) *Many Globalizations: Cultural Diversity in the Contemporary World*. Oxford: Oxford University Press.

Sunder Rajan, R. (1993) *Real and Imagined Women: Gender, Culture and Postcolonialism*. London and New York: Routledge.

Talwar, V. (1989) 'Feminist Consciousness in Women's Journals in Hindi: 1910–1920' in Sangari, K. and S. Vaid (eds) *Recasting Women: Essays on Colonial History*. New Delhi: Kali for Women.

Tanabe, A. and Y. Tokita-Tanabe (2003) 'Introduction: Gender and Modernity in Asia and the Pacific Gender and Modernity' in Hayami, Y. Tanabe A. and Y. Tokita-Tanabe (eds) *Perspectives from Asian and the Pacific*. Kyoto, Melbourne: Kyoto University Press and Trans Pacific Press.

Tenhunen, S. (1999) 'Urban Hierarchies in Flux: Arranged Intercaste Marriages in Calcutta' in Parpola, A. and S. Tenhunen (eds) *Changing Patterns of Kinship and Family in India: Proceedings from an International Symposium to Celebrate India's*

50 years of Independence at the University of Helsinki, 6 May 1998. Finnish Oriental Society.

Thapan, M. (2004) 'Embodiment and Identity' *Contributions to Indian Sociology* 38 (3): 411–444.

Tharu, S. and Niranjana, T. (1996) 'Problems for a Contemporary Theory of Gender' in Amin, S. And D. Chakrabarty *Subaltern Studies IX: Writings on South Asian History and Society.* New Delhi: Oxford University Press, pp. 232–260.

The Economist (2008) 'Tata Motors reveals its one-lakh car' [online]. Available at http://www.economist.com/business/displaystory.cfm?story_id=10498699 [Accessed on 10/08/08].

Thompson, J. B. (1996) 'Tradition and Self in a Mediated World' in Heelas, P., Lash, S. and P. Morris (eds) *Detraditionalization: Critical Reflections on Authority and Identity.* Cambridge, MA and Oxford: Blackwell.

Tokita-Tanabe, Y. (2003) 'Aesthetics of Female Self: Modernity and Cultural Agency of Urban Middle-Class Women in Orissa' in Hayami, Y., Tanabe, A. and Y. Tokita-Tanabe (eds) *Gender and Modernity: Perspectives from Asia and the Pacific.* Kyoto and Melbourne: Kyoto University Press and Trans Pacific Press.

Trautmann, T. (1993) 'The Study of Dravidian Kinship' in Uberoi, P (ed.) *Family, Kinship and Marriage in India.* Delhi: Oxford University Press.

Trinh, T. M. (1989) *Woman Native Other: Writing Postcoloniality and Feminism.* Bloomington: Indiana University Press.

Upadhya, C. (2007) 'Employment, Exclusion and "Merit" in the Indian IT Industry' *Economic and Political Weekly* 41 (36): 3865–3872.

Upadhya, C. and Vasavi, A. R. (2006) 'Work Culture and Sociality in the Indian IT Industry: A Sociological Study'. Final Report submitted to Indo-Dutch Programme for Alternatives in Development. Bangalore: National Institute for Advanced Studies.

Varma, P. K. (1998) *The Great Indian Middle Class.* New Delhi: Viking/Penguin.

Wajcman, J. (1998) *Managing Like a Man: Women and Men in Corporate Management.* Pennsylvania: The Pennsylvania State University Press.

Wallerstein, I. (2004) *World-Systems Analysis: An Introduction.* Durham: Duke University Press.

Williams, J. (2000) *Unbending Gender: Why Family and Work Conflict and What to Do About It.* Oxford: Oxford University Press.

Yuval-Davis, N. (1997) *Gender and Nation.* London and Thousand Oaks: Sage.

Appendix: Profiles of Interviewees

Anita, 32, has an MBA and is married with two children aged six years and six months, respectively, and works in a middle management position in Human Resources in a large Indian transnational company. She lives in a simple household with her husband, who is in a senior management position, and her children, but his grandmother has temporarily moved in to supervise childcare.

Anjali, 30, has eight years' work experience. She is currently working as a human resources manager in a large Indian transnational company. She lives in a nuclear household with her husband and a child aged two.

Anjana, 33, has an eight-year-old child and lives in a joint household with her husband, mother-in-law and parents. She has a degree in engineering and eleven years' work experience. She is currently a manager in the technical-writing division of a medium-sized transnational company.

Beena, 30, has seven years' experience and works in marketing at a junior managerial level with a medium-sized Indian transnational company. She is married and lives in a nuclear household.

Cristina, 29, is married to a lecturer in a college. She has two children aged five and one. She has a BSc in Computer Science and works at the administrative level in a reputed transnational company and has nine years' work experience. She lives in a nuclear household but her mother has temporarily moved in to help with the childcare.

Deepika, 27, a financial analyst, has six years' work experience and works for the offshore development centre of a well-known transnational company. She has a bachelor's degree in commerce and is currently completing her MBA. She is married and lives in a joint household with her husband who is in a similar line of work.

Geetika, 32, has two children aged five and one. She has a bachelor's degree in catering and eight years' work experience. She has recently taken up a (junior-level) operations management role in a large transnational company after a career break. Her husband is in a senior management position. They live in a nuclear household.

Hema, 26, is married to a software engineer. She works as an administrator in an established transnational company and has eight years' work experience. She completed her BSc degree via distance learning while working and is currently doing an MBA programme also via distance learning. She currently lives in a single-person household as her husband's job has taken him to another city.

Jaya, 33, is married and has a child aged five. She has a master's degree in Computer Application and works as the manager of a software maintenance team for a large transnational company. She is currently pursuing an executive

MBA programme. Her husband has a similar role in another transnational company. They live in a joint household which includes her grandmother.

Jyoti, 29, is married and has a one-year-old child. She works as a business development executive in a well-established transnational company. She currently lives in a nuclear household with her husband and child, but her mother or mother-in-law often visits to help with childcare.

Kanti, 35, has a Bachelor of Arts degree. She has seven years' work experience and is currently in an administrative position in a well-known transnational company. She lives in a joint household with her husband, who is unemployed, her child and her in-laws.

Lathika, 33, is single. She currently heads recruitment in the Offshore division of a medium-sized transnational company and has ten years' experience in the industry. Lathika has a master's degree in Social Work and is currently pursuing an MBA programme via distance learning. She lives with her parents.

Malini, 33, has a three-year-old child. She has an MBA in Human Resources and had about seven years' experience working with a large Indian transnational company when she took a career break to bring up her child. She currently lives in a nuclear household with her husband, a software engineer.

Maya, 37, is married and has a two-year-old child. She has a master's degree in Social Work and thirteen years' work experience. She heads the human resources division in the offshore development centre of a large transnational company. She lives in a nuclear household with her husband, who holds a senior position in the banking and financial sector, and her child.

Meenakshi, 24, has recently separated from her husband. She has about two years' work experience in the IT industry and a Bachelor of Arts degree. Harassment as a result of her ambiguous marital position caused her to give up her job as an executive in the human resource division of a medium-sized transnational IT company and to choose a similar role in the fitness industry. She lives in a working women's hostel.

Nalini, 37, has one child aged twelve. Her husband is a lecturer in a college and also has a part-time real estate business. With degrees in Social Work and Law and twelve years' experience, she is currently working as a junior manager in the legal division of the offshore development centre of an established transnational company.

Nitya, 27, is an executive financial analyst with a well-known transnational company. She is a qualified (chartered) accountant and has about three years' work experience. Her husband works in a similar area. She lives in a joint household with her husband and his parents.

Punita, 37, is married and lives in a nuclear household with her husband and two children aged eleven and eight. She works as a marketing executive in a well-established transnational company.

Rupa, 28, has been married for three years. She has an MBA and works as a human resource manager for a division of a large Indian transnational company with six years' experience. Rupa was born in Bangalore but her father's job as an employee of a public sector firm took the family to different parts of the country. She currently lives in a nuclear household with her husband, a software engineer.

Sarah, 36, is married and has eleven years' work experience. She works in a middle managerial level in business operations in an established transnational company. She is married and currently lives in a single-person household as her husband works elsewhere.

Savita, 32, has a four-year-old child. She has a degree in engineering and eleven years' work experience. She currently works in a senior management position in a large Indian transnational company, heading a team of over 150 people. Savita lives in a joint household which consists of her husband, a businessman, her mother-in-law and her child.

Shreela, 29, is a software engineer and works in a junior management position with a well-known transnational company. She has an engineering degree and nine years' work experience. She lives in a nuclear household with her husband who is also a software engineer.

Sumaiya, 29, has a two-year-old child and lives in a nuclear household with her husband who works with a charity. She has a Bachelor of Arts degree and works as a human resource executive in a large transnational company. She has about five years' work experience.

Swarna, 31, is married and lives in a joint household with her husband, her parents-in-law, her husband's grandmother and her child aged one. She works at a junior managerial level in the research and development section of a large transnational Indian company.

Swati, 34, has one child aged eight. She has a PhD in Computer Science and eight years' experience in the IT industry. She heads a software development team of about forty-five people for the offshore development centre of a transnational company. She currently lives with her daughter in Bangalore; her husband, a government employee whose job keeps him elsewhere, visits her often as do her in-laws.

Upasna, 28, is married. She works in an executive level in product development with a well-known transnational company. She lives in a nuclear household with her husband.

Index

Printed and bound by CPI Group (UK) Ltd, Croydon, CR0 4YY